The
People's
Prayer Book

The
People's
Prayer Book

Personal and Group Prayers

From RENEW International
Edited by
Carole Garibaldi Rogers and Mary Ann Jeselson

Liguori
LIGUORI, MISSOURI

Nihil Obstat:
Reverend Lawrence E. Frizzell, D.Phil.
Archdiocese of Newark Theological Commission
Censor Librorum

Imprimatur:
Most Reverend John J. Myers, D.D., J.C.D.
Archbishop of Newark

Published by Liguori Publications
Liguori, Missouri
www.liguori.org
www.catholicbooksonline.com

Library of Congress Cataloging-in-Publication Data

     The people's prayer book : personal and group prayers : from RENEW International / edited by Carole Garibaldi Rogers and Mary Ann Jeselson.

         p. cm.

     ISBN 0-7648-0986-5 (pbk.)

     1. Catholic Church—Prayer-books and devotions—English. I. Rogers, Carole G. II. Jeselson, Mary Ann. III. RENEW International.

BX2149.2 .P46 2003
242'.8—dc21   2002040655

Scripture quotations are taken from the *New Revised Standard Version Bible*, copyright 1989 by the Division of Christian Education of the National Council of the Churches of Christ in the U.S.A. Used by permission. All rights reserved.

English translation of the *Catechism of the Catholic Church* for the United States of America Copyright © 1994, United States Catholic Conference, Inc. — Libreria Editrice Vaticana. English translation of the *Catechism of the Catholic Church: Modifications from the Editio Typica* Copyright © 1997, United States Catholic Conference, Inc. — Libreria Editrice Vaticana. Used with permission.

Printed in the United States of America
07 06 05 04 03   5 4 3 2 1
First Edition

Contents

❧

Reaching Out 109

Letting Go 137

Asking Forgiveness 149

Prayers to Mary 159

PRAYER EXPERIENCES 165

Preface

~~~~

From the planning of the initial RENEW in 1976, prayer was seen as the basis for the entire spiritual renewal process. There was a clear acknowledgment that only God can change hearts. Personal renewal and renewal of the Church are entirely dependent upon the grace of God.

The emphasis on prayer was reflected in a number of ways. Literally, hours of prayer were put into staff meetings of those planning RENEW and the RENEW team itself as it formed. Prayer Networks were established across dioceses that involved motherhouses, centers of prayer, and seminaries, as well as daily prayer commitments by bishops, priests, and parishioners. Prayer, more than anything else, has been the driving force of RENEW's unexpected phenomenal growth to over 15,000 parishes in the

United States and twenty countries on six continents.

This emphasis on prayer continues with the very popular publication, *PRAYERTIME,* which offers reflections on the Sunday gospels for prayer and faith sharing. It is intended that *PRAYERTIME* be used at the beginning of each parish meeting, thereby creating a very positive and prayerful climate for more productive parish meetings. God's blessing is called upon for all parish ministerial planning and activity. The people at these meetings also go to Mass the following Sunday much better prepared to receive and embrace the proclamation of the gospel.

In this first ever collection of RENEW prayers, we offer prayers written, prayed, and pondered by RENEW staff members over the years. I am grateful to all the priests, religious, lay staff, and volunteers who contributed to this effort.

May this collection be for you a wonderful resource. Use it in your personal prayer but also in prayer with your families, small Christian communities, and parishes.

MSGR. THOMAS A. KLEISSLER
CO-FOUNDER, PRESIDENT
RENEW INTERNATIONAL

Introduction

Saint Paul wrote to the fledgling Christian community in Thessalonica, "Pray without ceasing." In the centuries since then, spiritual guides have noted that even if we pray always, we must also pray at specific times. We may pray in the morning and evening, before meals, or before meetings. Sometimes we use familiar prayers like the Our Father or the Hail Mary or even the *Magnificat*. Sometimes we pray wordlessly from deep within our hearts—a conversation felt rather than spoken. And sometimes we need other prayers—new combinations of thoughts and words that suit a particular event or emotion. For those times, RENEW International offers this collection of prayers.

The book is divided into three main sections. The first contains "Personal Prayers"—those that are appropriate for individuals. The second contains "Group Prayers"—those that might be used by a variety of gathered Christians, including couples, families, small Christian communities, and parish teams or committees. The third, "Prayer Experiences," is also meant for groups and contains prayers that involve some ritual or action that enhances the prayer.

You can use this book in many ways. Think of it as a basket filled with prayers. The prayers, like pieces of fruit, are arranged as we saw them. But you will select a prayer according to your taste, your need, the occasion, the season. In each of the first two sections there are further divisions—On the Journey, Reaching Out, Letting Go, Asking Forgiveness, and Prayers to Mary. We may have placed a prayer in one section—in "Letting Go," for example—but you may find it answers your need for a prayer of forgiveness. So do not be confined by our arrangement; explore all the sections. Similarly, in the "Group Prayers" section, you may find a prayer that suggests a role for a leader and a response from all; you might change that prayer into one all of you can pray together.

The largest component of both the personal and group prayers is called "On the Journey." Here we include prayers for all those times when prayer is essential, but we are so often at a loss for words, either because of our deep emotion or the seeming ordinariness of our days. Here you will find prayers for children we love, prayers about work, prayers in times of grief, and, quite simply, prayers for perseverance in the daily events of our lives. Throughout all sections, the titles of the prayers will help to identify some that are appropriate for a liturgical season, others for certain times or moods or petitions, still others for particular groups. Note that several prayers are especially for married couples—a category that is often missing in collections of prayers. Few prayers are designated specifically for praise or thanksgiving because the prayers in this collection, by and large, follow the model of our greatest prayer, the Our Father. They, too, begin with praise and end with petition.

Accompanying each of the prayers is a Scripture passage, which was chosen for that prayer. Most of these are from the gospels and many echo Sunday readings. You can start with a prayer that you selected for a particular reason and then read the Scripture passage. Or you might start with a particular Scripture reading and then use the accompanying prayer. Once again, it is your choice that will make this collection come alive.

These prayers have been selected from the more than 300 prayers written by RENEW International team members over the past 25 years. Some of the prayers first appeared in the IMPACT series, a collection of faith-sharing booklets that assist small Christian communities to carry out the mission of Christ. Some come from *PRAYERTIME, Faith-Sharing Reflections on the Sunday Gospels,* books that RENEW International has published for each of the three cycles of Sunday readings. And some come from Internet materials developed for ParishLife.com, RENEW International's pastoral Web site.

RENEW International took root in 1976 in the archdiocese of Newark. Its unique process of bringing parishioners together to reflect and pray has facilitated healing, spiritual renewal, and greater involvement in parishes across six continents. Since its beginning, RENEW has been guided and inspired by Msgr. Thomas A. Kleissler, who has written the Preface to this collection.

Throughout its history, RENEW International has been gifted with many talented, committed people who have provided ongoing reflection and leadership. These dedicated team members, including priests, laity, and religious, are the authors of these prayers. Hundreds, sometimes thousands, of people around the world have prayed them. This is, however, the first collection of RENEW prayers ever published.

We thank all the RENEW team members who have written these prayers over the years; without them, this book would not exist. We hope you will join all of us in prayer. In using this collection, may you find a deepening connection to God and to all God's people.

CAROLE GARIBALDI ROGERS AND
MARY ANN JESELSON, EDITORS

The
People's
Prayer Book

Personal Prayers

⚜

"Are any among you suffering?
They should pray.
Are any cheerful?
They should sing songs of praise."

JAMES 5:13

On the Journey

❦

To Follow God's Path

Loving Father,
the earth is full of your kindness,
which is in every step I take along the path
to the home you share with your Son, Jesus.
Open my eyes to see my many blessings.
Open my heart
to have confidence in your promise
and faith in the words of Jesus.
Free me from trying to create my own path
and help me to follow the path
you have placed before me.
Then my heart will not be troubled,
but will be filled with joyful peace.
These things I pray in confidence through
Christ our Lord.
Amen.

SCRIPTURE READING: JOHN 14:1–12

For Others on the Journey

Heavenly Father, I thank you
for the words, example, and actions
of your Son, Jesus,
which give us the path to follow.
I am grateful for the Spirit
who comes to be with us on our journey,
on the path of unity, forgiveness, care,
and love for one another.
Graced with the Resurrection of Jesus
and the Presence of the Spirit
help me to witness to others
as a member
of a community of baptized believers.
Amen.

SCRIPTURE READING: JOHN 20:19–31

For Enduring Faith

Lord, as Catholics
we are called to believe—
in the Trinity,
in the birth, death, and resurrection of Jesus,
in the "one, holy, catholic and apostolic"
church.
We are called to believe
that we are forgiven
and that we will rise again with you.
Lord, I sometimes struggle with these beliefs.
It is hard for me to keep things simple.
Life in this time and place
is complex
and its pressures intrude relentlessly.
Help me to listen for your voice,
to find you in others,
and to respond when you call me by name
as you called Mary Magdalene.
Help me on my journey
to grow ever closer to you.
Amen.

SCRIPTURE READING: JOHN 20:11–18

For Hope

Father, you created eyes to see,
limbs to move, ears to hear,
and life to be lived.
Help me to know our need for a word
of Good News
that touches all our senses
and energizes us to be a people of hope—
a hope that trusts
in what is promised.
I pray this in the name of the One
who was promised and now is with us
and for us,
Christ the Lord.
Amen.

SCRIPTURE READING: MATTHEW 11:2–11

Celebrating Our Humanity

Jesus, Word of God,
who has become flesh for our sakes,
help me celebrate the dignity of my humanity.
We are made in the image of God.
God chose our humanity
as the place of greatest intimacy
with creation.

Help me to share in this indwelling,
liberating love,
and let me proclaim your presence
as Word of God among us.
Amen.

SCRIPTURE READING: JOHN 1:1–18

For Stormy Times

Creator of the wind and sea,
storms and distractions abound
as we move through our daily lives.
When all around us is crashing and shifting,
we often lose our ability
to keep our eyes and hearts trained on you.
We forget who you are
and our faith becomes fragile.
During these times, bring to mind
the many ways you have been present to us
in the past,
and help us to experience your presence.
Forgive us when we doubt you,
and deepen our ability to trust.
I offer this prayer through Christ our Lord.
Amen.

SCRIPTURE READING: MARK 4:35–41

In Times of Weariness

Jesus, my shepherd,
sometimes the excitement of my ministry
is matched only by the fatigue
that creeps in upon me.
When I grow weary
help me to have the wisdom to stop,
even if briefly,
to sit a while with you and listen to you.
In my rest, open my eyes anew
to the many around me who need a touch,
a word, or a companion,
and grant me the grace to respond
with generous compassion
as I have seen you do.
Amen.

SCRIPTURE READING: MARK 6:30–34

For Attention to God's Word

Jesus,
your words have power
both to frighten and to delight me.
Help me be attentive, to hear
what you are teaching me about death
and about life.

Open my eyes to the challenges
you put before me.
Show me how to receive the "little ones."
Give me a generous spirit
and a compassionate heart.
I ask all of this in your holy name.
Amen

SCRIPTURE READING: MARK 9:30–37

To Walk With Others

Jesus, Son of Man,
you honored us with your presence
in this world during your life.
You will honor us with your presence again
at the end of this life.
I believe you are truly present
in the people around me,
and especially in those
whom you honored during your earthly life:
the poor,
the forgotten,
the sick and imprisoned,
those who are alone.
I can be with you when I am with them
in spirit,
in prayer,

in helping hands that lift up and comfort.
I ask you to walk with me.
In the quiet of my heart, allow me
to discover you.
Whenever and wherever I encounter you,
may I honor you
by whatever service I can give.
Amen.

SCRIPTURE READING: LUKE 21:25–28; 34–36

Healing Love

Lord Jesus,
You have gifted me with family and friends
who are so precious.
To love them warmly and unselfishly
gives me joy.
It helps me to recognize you
and be close to you.
You know so well the problems
that love can cause.
Your own life showed us
about the tough labor of love.
Help me care about the damage
that the wrong kind of love
can cause others—as well as myself.
Blessed be you, O Lord,

who has invited me
to share in your ministry of healing.
Amen.

SCRIPTURE READING: COLOSSIANS 3:12–17

Sharing God's Love

Father of our Lord Jesus Christ,
I rejoice
that you sent your Son to us.
As we wait for his return at the end of time,
we live in hope.
May our hearts be filled
with the joy you promised
when we live this life you gave us.
As a caring follower of Jesus,
help me to bring a sign of your love
to others in my life,
not that they may praise me,
but that they, too, may taste the joy
of the One
who is to come in glory.
I ask these things through Jesus
in the Holy Spirit.
Amen.

SCRIPTURE READING: LUKE 3:10–18

Easter Season

Faithful God,
I stand in astonishment at the empty tomb.
Your mercy and power,
evident in raising Jesus to life,
are more than I can comprehend.
Help me to receive with humility
the grace you offer to us
through Jesus' Resurrection and new life.
Direct me in the ways
I may, in turn, share this abundant grace
with all those around me.
With a full heart and in Jesus' name,
I offer you praise and thanksgiving
for the amazing love you pour out on us.
Amen.

SCRIPTURE READING: JOHN 20:1–9

Easter Season

Gracious God and Father,
the human heart is often slow to grasp
the impact of the Resurrection on all creation
and on our own lives as well.
When I doubt, give me
the comfort of your peace.

Strengthen me for the challenge
and the blessing of bearing your image.
Fill me with compassion and forgiveness
so that I reflect your image more clearly.
Help me to be a sign of Jesus' resurrected life
in my home, my parish, and my community.
With a full heart, and in Jesus' name,
I offer you praise and thanksgiving
for the amazing love you pour out on us.
Amen.

SCRIPTURE READING: JOHN 20:19–31

Pentecost

Most Holy Spirit,
you were present with the Father and the Son
when all of creation was called into being.
Your moving presence
took a small group of people
and made it into a new communion
that is your Church.
Make us worthy of your constant presence.
Divine Advocate,
direct my actions as an individual
and as a member of your Church
so that all I do

will reflect to the world
your love and presence, my God.
Amen.

SCRIPTURE READING: JOHN 14:15–16; 23B–26

Presence of the Spirit

O Holy Spirit,
by your overshadowing of Mary,
the gift of the Son of God was given
to our world.
Help me to appreciate the power
of your presence
when we gather as family, as Church,
and as community.
Give me a sensitivity to your gifts
wherever they are made manifest.
Help me to walk in your shadow,
which becomes clear
only in the light of Jesus, the Lord,
who lives and reigns with you and the Father,
forever and ever.
Amen.

SCRIPTURE READING: ACTS 1:12–14, 2:1–13

Living With the Spirit

Lord Jesus,
let your presence in my life
and the power of your Spirit
transform me and enable me
to choose living your kingdom
in my day and age,
and help me to remember
that I live in that presence
and with that Spirit.
Amen.

SCRIPTURE READING: LUKE 23:35–43

In Summer

Gracious God,
you provide for us always.
These early summer days explode
with the glory of greening and growing;
small seeds putting forth shoots,
and trees expanding their reach
as their canopies flourish and fill.
May they always be for me
physical reminders of the presence
of your kingdom.

May my hope be as constant
as the leaves that grow back
year after year.
And may that hope be a haven
for those who need rest.
With praise for the glory of these days
I offer my prayer in Jesus' name.
Amen.

SCRIPTURE READING: MARK 4:26–34

Placing God First

God of the living,
all the earth bows down before you.
All creation groans in praise of you.
You alone are the Lord of lords.
You alone are the God of all creation.
You invite all human beings
into deep and personal relationship.
You insist that we shall have no other gods
before you.
Help me as I seek to place you first in my life.
Send your Spirit to strengthen me
as I strive to embrace the cross,
and fill me with the wisdom I need
to resist the attachments of this world.

Alone I can do nothing;
with God all things are possible.
I ask this prayer through the power
of Jesus' name.
Amen.

SCRIPTURE READING: LUKE 14:25–33

Loving Day by Day

Jesus, it's hard to comprehend just how
privileged we are.
You have chosen us as your students,
your disciples,
and you want us to fully mature as teachers
of your Word and Way.
No matter what our job, our career,
and the daily tasks we embrace,
you want us to follow your Way
and represent you in every encounter
we have.
Please help me to spend
some of my best time each day
getting to know you better.
Help me learn how to love as you loved
and be an instrument of your love to others.

This I ask in your name,
you who live and reign with the Father,
and the Holy Spirit,
forever and ever.
Amen.

SCRIPTURE READING: LUKE 6:39–45

For Compassion

Compassionate God,
you adorn the earth with beauty,
and gift the world with abundant life.
You created human beings in your image
and you instill in them
your mercy and compassion.
Strengthen all your servants to grow
more fully in the divinity
you have shared with us,
so that we may offer your divine compassion
to those who are broken
by the losses and disappointments of life.
Instill in us the strength and the wisdom
to be prepared for your coming in our lives.
I ask this through Christ, our Lord.
Amen.

SCRIPTURE READING: LUKE 12:35–40

To Grow in Faith

Loving God and Father,
my life and support,
let me grow in faith,
and let me realize that my faith in you
is nothing in comparison
to your faith in me.
I ask this in the name of Jesus, my Brother,
who lives with you and the Holy Spirit,
one God, forever and ever.
Amen.

SCRIPTURE READING: LUKE 17:5–10

To Grow in Love

Father, I come before you
with a desire to grow in love.
Through your Son, Jesus, send your Holy
Spirit
to enlighten my mind and open my heart,
to grant me wisdom, hope, and peace.
May the Holy Spirit help me grow
in gifts of discernment, knowledge,
and compassion
so that I may serve you more completely.

May this same Spirit help me be present
to others,
responding to the Good News of your Son.
May my actions reflect his gospel of love,
today and always.
Amen.

SCRIPTURE READING: MATTHEW 5:13–16

Thanks for Blessings

What a great joy it is, O God,
to know you and to live
in the unending warmth of your love.
If you had only drawn me to yourself through
Jesus Christ,
it would have been far more than enough.
But you have also showered me
with earthly blessings:
freedom, prosperity, talents, friendships,
and much, much more.
Please lead me to use those blessings
in ways that fulfill your great purpose for me
in Christ,
so that I may be a blessing to others.
I pray in his name and in his Spirit.
Amen.

SCRIPTURE READING: 1 THESSALONIANS 5:12–18

Finding God

Lord,
you give us life and time
so that we can discover the warmth
and radiance of your love
in each other
and in what we do together.
Like Jesus, we have to do this
in a world open to good and evil.
Help me to recognize the joy
and the importance of my tasks,
to make my main activities
all that they can be
and in them to find you.
Amen.

SCRIPTURE READING: MARK 1:14–15

At Work

Loving God,
I am made in your image
and you are with me in my work,
in what I do for most of my waking hours.
In and through my work
I ask you to make me strong and protect me.

Give me your creative power and energy
to see that justice is done on earth
and light brought to all in darkness.
Amen.

SCRIPTURE READING: GENESIS 1:26–31

Witnessing the Gospel

God of power and might,
you teach us the marvels of the universe.
You have given us your Son,
the revelation of your divine presence,
and you invite us
into deep and everlasting relationship.
Help me
to grow in my desire to know you,
my hunger to be fed with your love,
and my longing to be imbued with the wisdom
of your Spirit.
Strengthen me
to become an effective witness of the gospel
and to promote your reign in the world.
I ask this through Christ, Our Lord.
Amen.

SCRIPTURE READING: LUKE 11:1–13

Growing Older

God, Our Father,
as I grow older, help me
to see the rest of my life
to be as important
as what has already occurred.
I know that your loving care
will be with me.
Enlighten me to move forward
with energy and purpose,
remembering Jesus' words,
"I came that they may have life,
and have it abundantly."
Help me continue to build
on the many blessings
you have bestowed on me,
and to see service and contribution
as vital to every stage of a Christian life.
I ask this through Jesus Christ
your Son, who lives with you
and the Holy Spirit,
one God forever.
Amen.

SCRIPTURE READING: GENESIS 12:4–5

Growing Older

O God,
you have made us in your image and likeness.
There is a purpose to our lives.
Help me to acknowledge the gifts
you have given me,
and to use them in your service.
I believe that you are still at work in me
And certainly there is so much
incompleteness all around us.
No matter how old I am,
may I always be aware of possibilities for good
and your call to make a difference.
I ask this through Christ our Lord.
Amen.

SCRIPTURE READING: JOHN 15:16

Growing Older

Lord, I am fearful about the future.
Even though I rejoice now
in the unique blessings
that come at this time of life,
I know some future hardships are inevitable.
Help me to trust in your loving care.
Enlighten and strengthen me

as the road gets steeper,
along my journey to heaven.
Amen.

SCRIPTURE READING: PHILIPPIANS 4:5–6

Growing Older

Faithful God,
you have given us yourself
in word and in sacrament
so that we may see you
with eyes of faith.
As I live out my days
help me to be an authentic reflection
of your presence within us.
Thank you for choosing to dwell
within and among us.
Grant me the courage and passion
to be a bearer of your peace
in a turbulent world.
In Jesus' name I pray.
Amen.

SCRIPTURE READING: JOHN 14:23–29

In Times of Grief

Lord, this road through grief
has lots of bumps, potholes, and detours.
I cry, "Where are you? I am lost."
Be with me now
even if I cannot feel your presence.
Guide me to the map of hope
so that I may see the light.
Help me to trust you to show me
the way out of this uncomfortable place.
Help me to find a way to connect
to your peace and love.
May your Spirit shine, even now.
I ask this in Jesus' name
and in union with the Holy Spirit.
Amen.

SCRIPTURE READING: PSALM 23

Reaching Out

ལྦོ∾

For Greater Awareness

Dear God,
I give you thanks
that I am made in your image and likeness.
Help me to be aware of your presence
in all your people.
Give me the courage to treat all
as I would treat Jesus.
I ask that your Holy Spirit open my heart
and teach me about your love
and my need to love others.
I truly desire to live Jesus' commands,
but am painfully aware that I cannot do it
without the help of your Spirit.
I ask this through our Lord and Savior,
Jesus Christ.
Amen.

SCRIPTURE READING: MATTHEW 5:38–48

For Courage to Love

Jesus, Lord and Giver of Life,
grant me the courage to love
those whom you love,
to seek out the rejected,
the alienated,
and the outsider.
Fill my heart
with the fire of your divine love
and soften my stony heart
so that the world may know
through me
that you love everyone.
Amen.

SCRIPTURE READING: MATTHEW 15:21–28

To Act With Justice

The earth is yours, O Creator,
and all that dwells therein is sacred.
There is nothing that exists
without your mark of divine love.
Enlighten my mind, open my heart,
empower me to act with justice.
Help me feed the hungry,
rather than hoard,

clothe the impoverished,
rather than consume,
give out of my wants and needs,
rather than oppress.
I pray that justice will reign
on the earth
and the light of your *shalom*
will break through the darkness.
I ask this through Jesus and in the Holy Spirit.
Amen.

SCRIPTURE READING: MATTHEW 22:15–21

To Care for Others

Lord of Life, empower me
with the guidance of your Spirit
to live in readiness for your coming
in the ways
I feed the hungry,
give drink to the thirsty,
shelter the homeless,
clothe the naked,
care for the sick,
visit prisoners,
bury the dead,
share knowledge of you,

give advice to those in need,
comfort those who suffer,
show patience to others,
forgive one another,
admonish those who need it,
pray for others.
Enliven my heart and guide my deeds.
In Jesus' name I pray.
Amen.

SCRIPTURE READING: MATTHEW 25:31–46

For Openness

Jesus,
I put my trust in your healing touch.
Unstop my ears and open my heart
to your message of justice, love,
and compassion,
even when those words challenge me.
Remove the impediments from my speech—
fear, intimidation, apathy, or doubt.
Help me to proclaim my faith loudly
and my love for you with gladness.
I pray all of this in your holy name.
Amen

SCRIPTURE READING: MARK 7:31–37

Easing Burdens

Dear God,
I praise and thank you
for Jesus who is your Word, your revelation.
Please help me to open my heart,
my mind, and my life
to your truth and your way.
Help me to accept my own burdens
and to be willing to work
toward easing the burdens of others.
I believe my life will be easy
and my burdens light
if I am joined to your Son
who is gentle and humble of heart.
Thank you for this great Incarnation
of your love.
In Jesus' name I pray.
Amen.

SCRIPTURE READING: MATTHEW 11:25–30

Moving Beyond Limitations

Lord our God,
it is your love that sustains us,
binds us to one another,
and call us out into the world.
Stretch me to move beyond
my own limitations
so that in all my actions
your love will be present
to bring about forgiveness, healing and justice.
With a grateful heart,
I thank you for your amazing love.
In Jesus' name, I pray.
Amen.

SCRIPTURE READING: JOHN 13:31–33A; 34–35

To Become a Good Shepherd

Loving Father, with a grateful heart,
I acknowledge the gift of your Son,
our Shepherd.
Help me learn to recognize his voice
when it is spoken to me every day,
but especially when I am vulnerable
and need protection and strength.
Give me the heart of a Good Shepherd,

that I, too, will care for those
who are vulnerable, anxious, lonely.
Help me to recognize myself in them
and to reach out to them in times of need.
I pray in union with the Holy Spirit,
through Christ our Lord.
Amen.

SCRIPTURE READING: JOHN 10:1–10

On the Road to Emmaus

Father in heaven,
you sent Jesus to die and rise,
to teach us and feed us.
Just as he was present
to the disciples of Emmaus
and their eyes were opened,
help me to recognize him this day
and each day as he walks with us.
Help me to follow his example
and to listen with care and compassion
to those in pain.
Give me the wisdom to respond as he would.
I ask this through Jesus and in the Holy Spirit.
Amen.

SCRIPTURE READING: LUKE 24:13–35

For Courage to Serve

God of our hopes and our dreams,
you have planted the hunger for glad tidings
within us.
Make your joy more complete
as we participate in proclaiming
this Good News;
the blind will see
the prisoner will be released.
Give us the courage
to reach out to the incarcerated
and bring into reality
this promise of freedom.
Help us to diffuse our fears
and know how to realize our call
so that a year of favor
may be celebrated in your name.
I pray this,
holding my reservations and anxiety
up to you,
and I ask for your blessing and grace,
through Jesus Christ, our Lord
and through your Holy Spirit.
Amen.

SCRIPTURE READING: LUKE 1:1–4; 4:14–21

For Compassion

Jesus, often I am so busy
that I don't even notice
those who are grieving around me,
those who are dead or lost.
And even when I do notice,
I am often afraid to reach out.
I don't know what to say
or what might be asked of me,
or where I will be led.
Forgive me for my misplaced priorities,
for my selfishness, and for my fear.
Open my eyes and touch my heart
so that I may respond
with your immediate and compassionate love
to those who are hurting around me.
Lead me into places
where people cry out for your mercy and healing
but are often ignored or punished vindictively.
Help me be the instrument
of your mercy and healing
and heal me in the process.
This I ask in your name,
You who live and reign with God the Father,
in the unity of the Holy Spirit, now and forever.
Amen.

SCRIPTURE READING: LUKE 7:11–17

For Mercy and Compassion

God of the lost,
through the Incarnation of your Son,
you free human beings from the ravages of sin,
and you pour out your abundant mercy
on the lost and the broken.
Sinners find refuge in the shadow
of your wings
and you provide your people
with an abundant harvest.
Send workers into the world
to seek out the lost
and offer life to sinners.
Direct my efforts and purify my heart,
as I go out seeking the lost sheep of this world.
May your Spirit empower me to become
a more effective ambassador
of your compassion.
I ask this in the name of Jesus, the Lord.
Amen.

SCRIPTURE READING: LUKE 15:1–10

For the Hungry

Generous God,
thank you for the home I have
and for the food on my table.
You alone know the hungers I bear
and how they can best be satisfied.
As I look to you for my nourishment,
open my eyes to the hungers around me
and, with the Spirit of Jesus,
give me the voice to call out the invitation,
"Come and eat!"
Amen.

SCRIPTURE READING: JOHN 21:1–14

For the Hungry

Our Father in heaven,
God and Father also of the hungry,
please care for them.
May we honor your holy name
by doing your will
regarding those who hunger.
As you give each of us each day
our daily bread,
we pray that our sisters and brothers
may be blessed in like manner.

Forgive us our sins of greed and indifference.
Lead us away from such temptation
and deliver us from the evil
of turning away from you and your children.
We pray in the name of Jesus,
Whose death and resurrection is our
everlasting hope.
Amen.

SCRIPTURE READING: EPHESIANS 4:22–25

To Become Bread for the World

Heavenly Father,
thank you for giving us yourself in Jesus,
through the Eucharist.
As we are fed by you,
open our eyes to see the hungry, the lonely,
and those in need of your presence.
By the grace of your Spirit,
may we live as the Body of Christ.
With grateful hearts, we offer the gifts we have
so that we may become bread
for the life of the world.
In Jesus' name I pray.
Amen.

SCRIPTURE READING: LUKE 9:11B–17

Love for All

Loving God and Father,
you have made me
in your image and likeness.
I believe that your very being is love.
Help me to accept your love for me
and for all your people,
even those who do not seem so lovable.
Fill my heart with your love,
so that I may become more loving
in all my thoughts and actions.
I ask this through Christ our Lord,
in the unity of the Holy Spirit.
Amen.

SCRIPTURE READING: GENESIS 1:27

For the Oppressed

Loving and gracious God,
You have called us to do justice
to those who are oppressed,
to share bread with them,
to pour ourselves out
for the hungry and afflicted,
and to break the yoke of oppression.
That's a tall order, God.
Thank you
for sending all of the prophets to us,
especially Jesus,
who incarnates your love
and shows us the way.
Please give me through your Holy Spirit
the strength, the wisdom, and the faith
to walk through the doors you open.
I ask this confidently
because of your amazing love for us
in Jesus Christ.
Amen.

SCRIPTURE READING: ISAIAH 58:3B–11

For Insight

Jesus, my Lord and friend,
help me to see the reality of my own life
and that of others,
as you do,
and share in your healing, loving work.
Open me to the fullness of your life and love
and grant that I may share life and love
abundantly.
Amen.

SCRIPTURE READING: JOHN 10:7–18

For Abundant Life

Loving God,
you have taught us
the value of human life through your Word.
Hear my plea to you
to open my heart and eyes to your love.
When your Son, Jesus,
came into the world,
the angels announced news of great joy.
During his lifetime, he told us he came
so that we might have life in great abundance.

Help me to become a bearer of that life
which Jesus came to bring.
I ask this in his name
and through the power of his Spirit.
Amen.

SCRIPTURE READING: ISAIAH 58:5–8

Letting Go

❦

Ordinary Moments

Father,
you come to us in our ordinary moments
to awaken us and call us toward a new reality
not of our own making.
Help me to be willing to let go
of what I seem to control
in order to be claimed as a disciple
of your Son.
Let me have a share
in your liberating and transforming ministry
through the power of the Holy Spirit.
Amen.

SCRIPTURE READING: MATTHEW 4:12–23

Finding God, Serving God

Lord, help me not to fear
poverty
sorrow
weakness
hunger
thirst.
We find you in our emptiness.

Lord, help me to seek
mercy
courage
peace
uprightness.
We serve you in our risk-taking.

Lord, help me to endure
persecution
lies
evil.
We witness you in our struggle.

And through it all we are blessed
as we become more like you.
Amen.

SCRIPTURE READING: MATTHEW 5:1–12A

To Grow in Trust

Loving and faithful Jesus,
I thank you for the generous gift of self
you have so willingly and totally sacrificed
for us.
You have modeled
what it means to be truly human,
accepting all that human living entails,
even death.
In plumbing the fullness of death,
you continually trusted in your Father,
relying on his love and fidelity.
Help me to develop that same trust in God,
to grow in the virtue of hope.
Be with me as I face
the constant deaths of daily existence,
as well as when I plumb the fullness
of my own death.
Be my constant companion and guide.
Lead me to continued life
united with the Father and the Spirit.
I ask this in continual trust and confidence,
now and forever.
Amen.

SCRIPTURE READING: MARK 14:1–15

For Courage in Discipleship

Jesus, brother and Lord,
your call to Peter
is echoed in my own call to discipleship.
At times I feel unsure
of how you could possibly desire me
for this service.
Yet, I know you can do great things
with my life
if only I consent.
Take my hesitancy and my reticence
and transform them into courage
and confidence in you.
Teach me how to respond wholeheartedly
to your invitation
and move more deeply
into intimate relationship with you.
I say yes to serving you and your people
in truth, justice, and mercy.
I pray this in your name.
Amen.

SCRIPTURE READING: LUKE 5:1–11

Challenges to Lifestyles

Jesus, you comfort the afflicted
and afflict the comfortable.
Help me to continue to open myself
to your challenging word and witness.
Give me the courage
to make hard decisions about my lifestyle,
and the compassion to embrace
those who are hurting
in our families and community.
Let me never forget
that your grace is sufficient.
You will never ask more than I can give
and you will always be walking with me.
This I ask in your name, Jesus Christ.
You live and reign with God our Father
in the unity of the Holy Spirit,
now and forever.
Amen.

SCRIPTURE READING: LUKE 6:17, 20–26

Unconditional Love

Jesus,
your witness of unconditional love
and forgiveness
is really difficult to follow.
Please help me as I struggle.
Don't let me become discouraged.
Help me to get back up each time I fail,
and to resolve more firmly
to be merciful and forgiving, as you were.
Help me to realize each day
that you have sent your Spirit of Love
to inhabit my heart
and to call on that Holy Spirit
each time I feel the fire of resentment
and retaliation building up inside.
Transform my hostile heart.
Transform our hostile society.
Amen.

SCRIPTURE READING: LUKE 6:27–38

In Times of Struggle

Jesus,
how often I find myself like Peter—
quick to call you Lord and Savior,
but slow to embrace your sacrificial
and saving Way.
I confess I am more comfortable
with your resurrection than with your passion.
Thank you, Jesus,
for your example of sacrificial love.
Thank you for your loving assurance
that my yoke will, indeed, be easy and my
burden light.
Help me to see my daily struggles
as opportunities to follow you
by embracing my cross and drinking my cup
as wholeheartedly as you did.
Help me to find sisters and brothers
willing to embrace this sacrificial calling
with me.
And whenever I cry out in my pain for mercy,
please send me the same consoling Spirit
who consoled you
in your moment of agony
in the Garden of Gethsemane.
I pray in your name, Jesus,
to our heavenly Father,

with whom you live and reign,
in the unity of the Holy Spirit, one God,
forever and ever.
Amen.

SCRIPTURE READING: LUKE 9:18–24

To Follow Jesus

Father of creation,
you have blessed each of us
with gifts of insight, feeling, and imagination.
I am grateful that I may bring these to prayer.
As I grow in an interior understanding
of your Son
I know you will bless me
even more completely
with the presence of the Spirit of your Son
who prays within each of us.
Filled with your gifts,
I come again and again to you,
confident that as I understand and love Jesus,
I will be moved to follow him closely.
I make this prayer through Jesus Christ,
our Lord.
Amen.

SCRIPTURE READING: JOHN 14:16–26

To Hear God's Word

Holy One of Israel,
You were rebuffed by your loved ones
who would not receive the prophet's call
through you.
I ache with your rejection.
I want to hear the challenges of the prophets
today
and respond wholeheartedly,
despite my fears of what this call may require.
I place myself at your disposal.
Direct me to the needs
you would have me address
so that your kingdom may come into being,
now and forevermore.
Amen.

SCRIPTURE READING: LUKE 4:21–30

Freedom From Possessions

Lord God, you came to set us free,
but materialism threatens to enslave us.
Give me the strength
to confront my own unreasonable desires.
Help me to take to heart your command
not to worry about what we are to eat
or what we are to put on.
Free me from worry about my possessions.
Help me to love people and use things,
rather than love things and use people.
Give me the grace
to embrace your whole vision of life,
to see your handiwork in all of your creation
and in all those I meet.
I ask this through Christ our Lord.
Amen.

SCRIPTURE READING: PSALM 139:13–16

To Learn to Love

Jesus, you tell us to love one another,
for in loving
we will be recognized as your disciples.
It is not always easy for me to love,
even those dearest to me.
My children's behavior can sometimes
drive me to distraction;
my spouse's actions sometimes
seem hurtful and unfair.
But when I look with loving eyes
and listen with loving ears,
I can see beyond the anger,
the frustration, and the hurt.
I can see your light in those eyes,
even though they may be filled with tears.
Help me, Jesus.
Help me to communicate with love
that I may come closer to you.
For as I learn to speak and to listen
with love in my heart
I help to build a more peaceful world,
in your name.
Amen.

SCRIPTURE READING: 1 CORINTHIANS 14:6–12

Asking Forgiveness

God's Healing Presence

God of mercy and justice,
you give us so many examples
of your healing presence in Scripture,
in our daily lives,
in the events of history.
Thank you for the incredible gift
of your presence
in the person of Jesus
and his intimate union with us
through the Eucharist.
How lavish your love is!
I acknowledge and confess my lack of faith,
my lack of love,
and my lack of courage
for being your instrument of healing
in my own time.

Open my eyes, deepen my faith.
Send your Spirit of love and courage
to pray and work for the healing
of suffering individuals
and for the healing of our suffering society
and world.
I ask this in the name of Jesus Christ, our
Lord.
Amen.

SCRIPTURE READING: LUKE 7:1–10

Forgiving Others

Jesus, you forgave your killers
even as they nailed you to the cross.
Teach me to forgive,
to forget myself in love,
to take the tremendous risk of letting go.
Send your Spirit into my life
to move my heart
and shape my soul
so that I might forgive those
who have sinned against me.
Amen.

SCRIPTURE READING: MATTHEW 18:21–35

New Patterns

Faithful God, in baptism
you made us partners
in the new covenant of love
that you established in Jesus, your Son.
Strengthen me to turn away
from old patterns of sin,
open me to the newness of life you offer,
and renew my commitment
to share your mission
or to serve others.
I ask this through the same Christ our Lord.
Amen.

SCRIPTURE READING: MARK 2:18–22

To See Anew

Heavenly Father,
I ask you to keep me from taking
the ordinary so much for granted.
Help me to be patient with others.
Help me to appreciate all people
and see anew the mystery of godliness
within them.
Give me humility
to ask for the forgiveness I need
and the generosity to offer my own forgiveness
to others in return.
I ask this through your Son, Jesus Christ,
in union with the Holy Spirit.
Amen.

SCRIPTURE READING: LUKE 2:41–52

Growing in God's Love

God of mercy, Father of all,
you welcome the downtrodden
and are a voice for the voiceless.
You feed the poor
and offer forgiveness to sinners.
And, above all, you sent your Son
for the salvation of the world.

Reveal to me my unrepentant, stony heart
and replace it
with a heart full of love and compassion.
Place your Spirit within me,
so that I might walk in your footsteps
and speak your word to a waiting world.
Enfold me in your protective arms
and help me grow in the intimacy
you long to share with me.
I ask this through Christ, our Lord.
Amen.

SCRIPTURE READING: LUKE 13:20–30

For Gratitude

Almighty God,
I am grateful to you for my existence.
I am sorry for the complaints
you often hear from me.
In fact, "my cup overflows."
Help me to live your gift of life
to the fullest
each day of my life.
Amen.

SCRIPTURE READING: LUKE 17:11–19

For Guidance

O God,
when it comes to hunger,
your love truly covers a multitude of sins.
There is so much I have failed to do.
I ask you to forgive me for Jesus' sake.
I ask you to show me more clearly
what it is you would have me do next.
Help me to take a few steps forward
and help me to do so
as a way of thanking you for your great love
in making me your child through Jesus Christ,
our Lord.
Amen.

SCRIPTURE READING: 1 THESSALONIANS 5:12–18

For Greater Awareness of Others

Lord, you gave all women and men
an incomparable dignity
as your own partners.
Forgive me for the times
I have made people just tools
for my own purposes.

Help me open my eyes
to the people I work with
and their needs and struggles,
so that I may discover both them and you.
I pray this prayer in Jesus' name.
Amen.

SCRIPTURE READING: PHILIPPIANS 2:1–11

Bad Choices

Lord, I am indeed a "work in progress"
and as long as I am alive
I will make some bad choices.
At times, I turn away from you and your love.
Help me to remember that,
even then, you are with me.
I can be forgiven.
Help me to understand
that admitting my wrongs
and trying to do better
are all that you ask of me.
Help me, Lord, to see
that when I truly know your love,
I can truly forgive myself.
Amen.

SCRIPTURE READING: LUKE 15:11–24

Turning Away From Revenge

God of earth, sea, and sky,
God of plants, animals, and persons,
you alone have power over life and death.
Cleanse my heart of all feelings of revenge.
Change my heart of stone
to a heart of flesh
so that I may recognize your image
in all persons, regardless of their deeds.
I make my prayer through Christ our Lord.
Amen.

SCRIPTURE READING: MATTHEW 5:21–24

Choosing Life

Loving God and Father,
giver of life,
lead me to see evil wherever it resides,
even in our laws and government.
Help me always to choose life over death.
Help me to see mistakes that we all make
and, at the same time,
help me to forgive as your Son taught us,
not seven times but seventy times seven.
I ask this in the name of Jesus,

who lives and loves with you
and the Holy Spirit,
forever and ever.
Amen.

SCRIPTURE READING: LUKE 23:32–35

Everyday Forgiveness

How many times do I have to tell you
something?
How often do I have to remind you?
How many times have I asked you not to do
that?
How long do you expect me to keep asking?

How many times, Lord, have I asked those
very questions?
I don't like your answer:
not seven times, but an infinite number
of times.
Lord, sometimes it is more difficult
to forgive the constant aggravations
than to forgive the truly big hurts.
Provide me with patience
and teach me forgiveness this day.
Amen.

SCRIPTURE READING: MATTHEW 18:21–22

Trying to Change

God,
you have taught us the way of forgiveness.
Help me in my feeble efforts to be like you.
Once again, I plead with you
to change my stony heart to a heart of flesh.
Help me to understand better your people and
myself.
I thank you for the insights
I have received from prayer and from others.
Help me to realize that the power
of forgiveness
will always prevail over the power of violence.
Be with me as I try to change.
Amen.

SCRIPTURE READING: LUKE 23:32–34A

Prayers to Mary

❧⌣❧

For Help on Ordinary Days

Mary, you are the Mother of Jesus
and my Mother,
my guide and inspiration.
Although I see your life as extraordinary,
you lived each day as an ordinary person
in your own time and place.
Help me to live my own ordinary life
according to God's will.
Help me to see God's will
and the connections between the ordinary
and extraordinary
that happen for me each day.
Give me the commitment
to ponder and savor life as you did.

Bless me with insight to recognize
the Spirit's action in my life
and reflect the Father's goodness to others.
I ask this in the name of Jesus, your Son.
Amen.

SCRIPTURE READING: LUKE 2:16–21

To Pray and Ponder

Mary, pray that I might treasure life
beauty
goodness
opportunity
truth.

Mary, pray that I might ponder
how to defend life
how to see and hear beauty
how to affirm and share goodness
how to grasp and utilize opportunity
how to seek and proclaim truth.

Mary, pray that I treasure what I have
and ponder what I might become.
Amen.

SCRIPTURE READING: LUKE 2:16–21

Contemplation and Action

Mary, you are both the Mother of God
and our mother.
Help me to find in your life
of faithful discipleship
a model for my own life.
Help me to reflect on your role
as both Mother and follower of Jesus
and to see in the gospel stories
both your contemplative spirit
and your faith in action.
Help me to look around me
with compassion, to turn to your Son
in prayer, and trust in his response.
Help me to live always
with the Spirit in my life.
I ask this through our Lord Jesus Christ,
your Son,
who lives and reigns with God the Father
and the Holy Spirit,
one God forever and ever.
Amen.

SCRIPTURE READING: JOHN 2:1–12

Help in Saying Yes

Mary, as I ponder your life,
help me recall the many ways
and the many times
you showed your love.
Help me remember your attention to prayer
as a faithful Jewish wife and mother,
your generous yes to God,
your attentiveness toward others,
your courage in difficult times,
your Spirit-filled discipleship.
Help me welcome your presence in my life
as role model, companion, mother.
Help me live as a faith-filled disciple
always ready to follow your Son,
always ready to say my own yes.
I ask this, as always, through your Son,
Jesus Christ, who lives and reigns
with the Father and the Holy Spirit,
forever and ever.
Amen.

SCRIPTURE READINGS: JOHN 19:25–27; ACTS 1:14

Waiting by Faith

O Mary, model of a faith-filled life,
you were committed
to turning all things over to your Lord
and Maker.
Help me to imitate your *fiat* prayer.

"Let it be with me
according to your word."

When annunciations from God
leave questions and wonderment,
help me to know down deep
that I, like you, am always totally dependent
on God.
Loving handmaid of the Lord,
you can teach me
to "wait by faith and not by sight."
I ask your prayerful assistance
as I direct my prayer
to the Father, through Jesus,
the Son of God and your Son
by the Spirit's overshadowing.
Amen.

SCRIPTURE READING: LUKE 1:26–45

Group Prayers

*"For where two or three are gathered
in my name,
I am there among them."*

MATTHEW 18:20

On the Journey

❧⟊❧

RENEW Prayer

Gracious God and Father, we are your people
embraced by your love. We thank you for your
presence with us throughout all time.
Create us anew through Jesus Christ your Son.
Liberate us from all that keeps us from you.
Send your Holy Spirit, enabling us
to share in your work
of recreating our world and restoring justice.
Heal us from every form of sin and violence.
Transform us to live your Word more
profoundly. Reconcile us so enemies become
friends. Awaken us to the sacred; nurture our
relationships. Enliven our parishes; reunite
our families. Fill us with joy to celebrate the
fullness of life. Empower us to be a community
of love growing in your likeness by the grace
of Christ our Lord.
Amen.

Seasons of Life

Leader: When it is the springtime of our life
   together, we pray:

All: Our time of solitude has passed;
   we move to the warmth
   of the newly-returned sun.
   New life, new beginnings,
   we start out on our journey together,
   ready to share, to grow, and to love.

Leader: When it is the summer of our life
   together, we pray:

All: We are called to move outside,
   to go beyond ourselves.
   As all things are growing,
   so are we, in faith, in hope, and in love.

Leader: In the autumn of our life together,
   we pray:

All: The harvests are gathered,
   the colors of the earth are changing.
   We have seen more,
   and look at one another with wiser eyes.

Leader: And when the winter arrives, we pray:

All: Our spirits move in quiet and
   contemplation.
   We slow our pace and relax into the
   darkness,

for we know that, in this place,
much growth occurs.
The strength of our love warms us
until we feel again, the warmth
of the springtime sun.

All: Amen.

SCRIPTURE READING: EPHESIANS 3:16–19

Seasons of Life

For this antiphonal prayer, divide the group into two parts.

Leader: For everything there is a season
and a time for every matter
under heaven.

Side 1: A time to be born,
Side 2: and a time to die;
Side 1: a time to plant,
Side 2: and a time to pluck up what is planted;
Side 1: a time to kill,
Side 2: and a time to heal;
Side 1: a time to break down,
Side 2: and a time to build up;
Side 1: a time to weep,
Side 2: and a time to laugh;
Side 1: a time to mourn,

Side 2: and a time to dance;
Side 1: a time to throw away stones,
Side 2: and a time to gather stones together;
Side 1: a time to embrace,
Side 2: and a time to refrain from embracing;
Side 1: a time to seek,
Side 2: and a time to lose;
Side 1: a time to keep,
Side 2: and a time to throw away;
Side 1: a time to tear,
Side 2: and a time to sew;
Side 1: a time to keep silence,
Side 2: and a time to speak;
Side 1: a time to love,
Side 2: and a time to hate;
Side 1: a time for war,
Side 2: and a time for peace.

All: God, Source of all life,
we pray that we may come
to accept and honor all those times,
both the joyful and the sad,
the easy and the unpleasant—
the light and the dark sides of life.
It is in this paradox
that we come to know you,

and in knowing you,
we find the love
for which we are always searching.
Bring us to that love
through the sacramental graces
earned for us by your Son, Jesus Christ,
and through the power of your Holy Spirit.
Amen.

SCRIPTURE READING: ECCLESIASTES 3:1–8

For Spiritual Growth

Gracious God and Father,
aware and appreciative
of a growing sense of spirituality in our world,
we thank you again for our Christian way
of coming to know and love you.
Bless us in our spiritual growth.
May we have a sense of balance
that empowers us to be contemplative
and active.
May we know and practice a prayer
that leads us ever more closely to you,
into our communities, and out to our world.

May we faithfully reflect
upon our spiritual experience
so we may better understand
both you and ourselves,
so we may love, as Jesus taught us:
God,
others,
and ourselves.
We make our prayer through our Lord Jesus
Christ,
who lives and reigns with you
and the Holy Spirit,
one God, forever and ever.
Amen.

SCRIPTURE READING: COLOSSIANS 3:1–4, 12–17

Being Present to Each Other

Loving Father, through your Son, Jesus,
you call us to gather as your people,
holy and beloved.
As we come into your presence,
open our hearts to your love,
open our minds to your truth.
Help us to be present to each other
and to you
as we pray.

Grant this through our Lord, Jesus Christ,
your Son, who lives and reigns with you
and the Holy Spirit,
one God, forever and ever.
Amen.

SCRIPTURE READING: JOHN 10:1–15

Embracing Others

Lord our God,
thank you for bringing us
into the love relationship
that exists in your being from all eternity.
We humbly offer you ourselves in return,
and ask that you use us as you will
in the work set before us.
As you embrace us in solidarity,
help us to embrace those around us
who are alone and in need
of your living presence.
We offer this prayer,
in the name of the Father,
and of the Son
and of the Holy Spirit.
Amen.

SCRIPTURE READING: JOHN 16:12–15

Using Our Gifts, Empowering Others

Lord God, we gather together in your name.
We acknowledge your loving presence
among us.
We ask you to help us to recognize
the many gifts we have received from you.
We thank you, in particular,
for inviting us to serve you.
Guide us
as we seek to use our own gifts more fully
and to empower others to use theirs.
Be with us
as we deepen our understanding
of all that you call us to be.
We ask this through your Son, Jesus Christ,
who lives and reigns with you
and the Holy Spirit,
one God, forever and ever.
Amen.

SCRIPTURE READING: 1 CORINTHIANS 12:4–12

Everyday Work

God, Creator of all life,
thank you for the gift of life.
Help us to find you, delight in you,
in the kindness and love we give and receive.
Help us to do our job as Christians,
to show where you can truly be found.
Give us clarity of vision and your vision
to be conscious of how our daily work
affects us and others.
Send your Holy Spirit upon us now
that we may be open and honest
with each other
so that we may truly grow to full maturity
in Christ Jesus.
Amen.

SCRIPTURE READING: EPHESIANS 4:1–7, 11–13

Advent

Leader: In the night,
All: Come, Lord Jesus.
Leader: In the cold,
All: Come, Lord Jesus.
Leader: As we wait,
All: Come, Lord Jesus.
Leader: As we tire,
All: Come, Lord Jesus.
Leader: Into our hearts,
All: Come, Lord Jesus.
Leader: Into our lives,
All: Come, Lord Jesus.
Leader: Into our world,
All: Come, Lord Jesus.
Leader: This Advent, we pray that we might wait in joyful hope for the coming of our Savior, Jesus Christ.
All: Amen.

SCRIPTURE READING: MATTHEW 24:37–44

Living Faith

Spirit of the Living God,
captivate our imagination,
empower our will,
energize our spirit
so we will learn to take our inner convictions
and live them out more fully day by day.
Jesus, Savior and companion,
strengthen our determination
to follow your way of service,
to open our hearts to forgive,
to embrace searcher, sinner, and saint alike
so we will integrate your way, your truth,
and your life into our lives.
God our Father and Creator,
source of all that is,
grace us to live your way of love
as we meet one another
on this journey of faith.
Blessed be your name.
Amen.

SCRIPTURE READING: MATTHEW 23:1–12

To Affirm Others

Blessed are you, Lord God of all creation
and Father of us all, for the gift of your Son
who has shown us what it means to be human.
His presence in our midst
infinitely ennobles our human dignity
and worth
beyond anything imaginable.
We thank and praise you
for that magnificent gift.
Like your Son, let us walk among one another
as your sons and daughters,
members of the same family.
Let us always affirm the dignity and worth
of every human being,
and give us the grace and the strength
when such affirmation is difficult for us.
We ask this through your Son, Jesus,
and in the Holy Spirit.
Amen.

SCRIPTURE READING: MARK 16:15–20

For Awareness of God's Presence

God of all times, you alone know the time
when Christ will return in glory.
We thank you for bringing us together
around your Word.
Set our hearts on using well
the time you have given us on earth.
Keep us alert to your presence
in those around us, and fill us with hope
as we strive to live in your reign.
We ask this through Christ our Lord.
Amen.

SCRIPTURE READING: MARK 13:33–37

Following the Right Path

Loving God,
Jesus taught us so many lessons
during his time on this earth.
As we come together to search out
these lessons,
we come with open hearts and minds.
Open our hearts and minds
that we may see the goodness
you have put
in the highways and byways of our life.

Keep us attentive to your words
that our footsteps and actions may follow
the same path,
the path that Jesus shows,
the path we claim to be walking.
Guide our feet that they may stay on the path
of the gospel,
the way that Jesus the teacher has shown us.
We ask this through the same Christ, our
Lord.
Amen.

SCRIPTURE READING: MARK 1:21–28

Responding to God's Call

Gracious God, in Jesus' words
we are invited
to be partners in his work
of witnessing to your kingdom on earth.
In his words,
we are reminded of the mission and
responsibility
that we received in our baptism.
Keep our hearts, eyes, and ears open,
so that daily we will respond to your call.

With courage and humility,
relying on your grace,
may we be agents of healing,
bearers of truth,
and messengers of hope.
We offer this prayer through Jesus Christ
our Lord.
Amen.

SCRIPTURE READING: MARK 6:7–13

For the Heart of a Child

God of love and compassion,
it is not always easy to hear
what you expect of us.
It is difficult to live out our commitments
and sometimes we fail.
Help us to trust
in your forgiveness and understanding,
especially when we fail to live up to the ideals
you place before us.
We believe in your goodness and mercy.
We place ourselves
and all those who struggle
to remain faithful in their relationships
into your compassionate care.

Give us the heart, the mind, and the spirit
of the little child
who looks to you clear-eyed and hopeful.
We pray all of this in the name of our Lord,
Jesus Christ.
Amen.

SCRIPTURE READING: MARK 10:2–16

The Love of a Shepherd

Leader: "My sheep hear my voice…"
All: Lord Jesus, help us to follow you faithfully
and offer assistance
to our brothers and sisters
who may wander.
Leader: "I give them eternal life…"
All: Lord Jesus, teach us to know the ways
we can begin to live and share eternal life
while in this world.
Leader: "The Father and I are one."
All: Lord Jesus, thank you for sending your
Holy Spirit
to bring us into the intimacy
of your relationship with the Father.
Enlarge our hearts
to embrace those who have wandered
from you

and help us to love and protect them
with the heart of a shepherd.
Amen.

SCRIPTURE READING: JOHN 10:27–30

The Gift of Speech

Spirit of Truth,
come be with us as we pray.
We give thanks for the gifts of speech
and communication.
We know it is within our power
to change what we need to change.
Knowing that we often fail as
instruments of your peace,
give us direction and power.
Give us the inspiration to support
one another as we walk this journey
together with you.
We ask this in the name of Jesus,
our companion,
who lives with the Father
and you forever.
Amen.

SPIRITUAL READING: LUKE 6:43–45

For Compassion and Patience

Lord, teach us never to take those we love
for granted.
Lead us to laugh with those who laugh
and weep with those who weep,
to be truly with them in presence
and in spirit,
in joyful times and in sad times.
Give us the patience, Lord,
to allow your plan to unfold in our lives.
Sometimes this may mean struggling
with the anguish and suffering
that accompanies the illness of another
or even our own pain.
As we help others carry their crosses,
as we humbly allow others
the privilege of helping us to bear ours,
may we always allow your grace
to enfold us.
Lord, through these experiences,
you might call forth from us
the tenderness we need to be human,
the compassion we need to be Christ-like,
the love we need to say yes
to all you ask of us.
Hear us, Father, through Jesus your Son,

who accepted our humanity in its fullness
that one day we might share in his
and your divinity,
forever and ever.
Amen.

SCRIPTURE READING: MATTHEW 11:28–30

For a Loving Community

Leader: We remember God's presence
as we gather to pray.
All: Jesus, you showed us
how a community should live.
Loving and caring and helping
one another were the cornerstones.
We need to remember
that we can help to create community.
We can come together
and share with one another,
support one another, and love one another.
It may seem difficult in these times,
but your example shows us the way.
Guide us, dear Jesus, for we need your help.
We ask this in your name.
Amen.

SCRIPTURE READING: ACTS 2:46

The Gift of Community

For this antiphonal prayer, divide the group into two parts.

Side 1: We need one another, Lord,

Side 2: even though we are taught to go it alone.

Side 1: We need help, Lord, from you and from each other

Side 2: even though we must stand on our own two feet.

Side 1: We need to be with one another, Lord,

Side 2: even though we must find our own way.

Side 1: Lord, we need to laugh and cry together

Side 2: for it is then that we truly experience your love.

All: We praise and thank you for the gift of friends, family, and community.
Help us to recognize these gifts,
so that we may share our lives and our love,
and thus make our small part of this world
a better place.
Amen.

SCRIPTURE READING: ACTS 2:46

Called to Your Table

Jesus, we call you the Bread of Life.
We are reminded of your sacrifice for us
each time we receive the Eucharist.
Call us to your table
as we bring with us
all of our triumphs and joys,
hurts and disappointments,
all of our tears and pain
as well as our laughter.
We give everything to you,
our sacrifice mingled with yours.
For this is true communion;
this is how we come together,
the beginning of our knowing you.
Help us to be an example to children.
Open us up to their simple faith.
Give us wisdom, joy, and peace
as we try to grow ever closer to you.
We ask this in your name.
Amen.

SCRIPTURE READING: JOHN 6:52–71

Food for Life

Lord, in John's Gospel,
we hear you say,
"Do not work for the food that perishes."
Lord, we know the food we need for life.
We do not fully understand
the mystery of your becoming present to us
in the Eucharist,
but we struggle to believe.
Your words help us to see
where we need to put our energies:
toward knowing you
and living as you would have us live.
We need help to avoid working
for those things that cannot last.
We need help to remember
what is really important in life.
Help us to be faithful to the Eucharist,
so that we may come to be more
in communion with one another and you.
Amen.

SCRIPTURE READING: JOHN 6:25–35

Right Relationships

Loving God and Father,
in your wisdom you gave your Son,
Jesus, to Mary and Joseph
so they could nurture, love, protect,
and guide him in his early years.
Guide us, and strengthen us
in our relationships with our families.
Father, you taught us, through Jesus,
that we are all your sons and daughters.
Help us, Lord,
to enter the world each day
with respect and compassion
for the sisters and brothers we will meet.
We ask all this through Jesus,
and in the power of the Holy Spirit.
Amen.

SCRIPTURE READING: LUKE 2:41–52 OR MARK 3:31–35

For All Families

God of radiant light,
you spoke to Moses through the burning bush.
You led the people through the desert
by a pillar of fire.
And you sent the purifying fire of your Spirit
to renew and transform the earth.
Strengthen our families
as we face the seductions of this world.
In these days of fulfillment, purify us
so that when the test comes,
families will stand united
in their choice of you.
And in our own baptism by fire,
give us the grace to withstand
the trials of our lives,
so that, like gold purified by fire,
we, too, may be fashioned
in your brilliant image.
We ask this through Christ, our Lord.
Amen.

SCRIPTURE READING: LUKE 12:49–53

For All Families

Thank you, God, for our own families
and for the many faces of family
we encounter each day.
Give us your wisdom
to encourage and strengthen
good family values.
Endow us with the virtues
of heartfelt compassion,
kindness, humility, gentleness, patience,
forgiveness,
and teach us to bear with one another
in a loving and just way.

> *[Here invite each person to add a prayer for
> his or her own family members and family
> needs. Conclude by praying the closing line.]*

We make this prayer in Jesus' name.
Amen.

SCRIPTURE READING: COLOSSIANS 3:12–17

For Our Families

Lord, God, who gave life to each of us
within our own special family,
we thank you for the gift of each other.
We remember those of our grandparents
and great grandparents and others
who have died.

[Pause. Mention by name if you wish.]

We thank you for the goodness they brought
to our family.
We thank you, too, for parents,
children, and grandchildren,
for all of us here today.
We pray for all our extended families
—aunts, uncles, cousins, and in-laws.

[Change as appropriate for each family.]

Let us always remember where we come from
—and where we are going.
We thank you for the memories
of the past that we cherish.
Bless us in the present.
Help us to show your grace to each other,
so your glory may shine ever brighter
in our family and in our world.

We ask this through Jesus Christ, your Son,
in union with the Holy Spirit.
Amen.

SCRIPTURE READING: LUKE 11:1–8

For Groups of Families Gathered Together

Lord God,
as we gather together in your name,
let us always remember to praise you
and thank you.
We thank you for the gift of friendship,
which brings us together.
We thank you for our Church,
which holds us together.
We thank you for this opportunity
to remember our heritage.
We thank you for the food we are about to share,
for the surroundings where we celebrate.
We ask your blessing on all the families here,
on all the members of their families.
Help each of us to remember
both our family heritage
and our Christian heritage

so that we will have the strength and courage
to live out our baptismal promises
and serve you.
We ask this through Jesus Christ,
your Son, in union with the Holy Spirit.
Amen.

SCRIPTURE READING: LUKE 11:9–13

To Be Good Parents

Lord, the news these days seem
to be more bad than good.
We can easily get caught up
into thinking that things are hopeless.
There seems to be much
from which we need to protect our children.
Our faith, however, can keep us strong.
Our belief in you means belief
in a better world,
a better way to be.
We are trying to be Christian parents.
We know that we are called
to live out Christian principles,
even though we are surrounded
by a culture that tempts us
to do just the opposite.

With your help, we can withstand the
pressures and help our children
to do the same.
Our example teaches more than words
ever could,
and we ask for the strength to stand firm.
We need to remember, too,
that there is much good in the world.
Help us to see it, and to affirm and support
those who are signs of hope and goodness.
We ask this in your name.
Amen.

SCRIPTURE READING: JOHN 20:11–18

For Married Couples

Loving God and Father,
we gather together to begin a journey
with you and with one another.
Help us to make it a journey
toward deeper understanding and love,
toward a more faith-filled
commitment in our lives.
Remind us always to walk gently,
with respect and acceptance
for our differences,

and with joy in our mutual desire
to build a better world for our children.
We ask this in the name of Jesus,
our brother, and through the Holy Spirit.
Amen.

SCRIPTURE READING: COLOSSIANS 3:12–17

For Married Couples

Dear God and Father of our families,
as you nourish, sustain, and nurture us,
teach us
how to nourish, sustain, and nurture
our children.
Give us listening hearts,
open to hear you and to hear our children.
Unite our families;
heal our wounded hearts;
deepen our faith.
Help us to make you visible through our love.
We ask this through Jesus
and in the power of the Holy Spirit.
Amen.

SCRIPTURE READING: COLOSSIANS 3:12–17

For Married Couples

Jesus, our brother,
you encounter us in a special way
in the sacrament of marriage.
You bestow upon us the graces
which strengthen our relationship.
Sometimes, however, it is not easy
to remember your presence.
Help us, Lord, to keep in mind
that you are indeed with us
and a part of our marriage relationship.
Strengthen us, in love, to remember that
you brought us together for a reason:
that we need to honor each other
and each other's emotions.
Continue to remind us of your presence
as, together, we fulfill our marriage vows
until death.
Amen.

SCRIPTURE READING: 1 CORINTHIANS 13:4–7, 13

For Married Couples

Loving God and Father, out of love for us
you sent your only Son, Jesus,
into the world to save us
and to teach us how to love.
But sometimes
we just do not feel like loving each other.
We cannot find the energy to make this
relationship work.
We need your grace.
Help us to make love the center of our lives.
Grant us the virtues of patience and kindness,
trust and hope.
We pray that we can make our marriage
endure,
as a living testament to you
who live forever with Jesus,
our brother, and the Holy Spirit
in one loving community.
Amen.

SCRIPTURE READING: 1 CORINTHIANS 13:4–7, 13

For Married Couples

As we come together, dear God,
we bring our different backgrounds,
our different experiences, our different lives.

*[Pause for a moment to reflect on life
before marriage.]*

We hope that in our listening to your Word,
and in our sharing,
we realize what is truly important in our lives.
Help us to see that our differences
are not so much problems to overcome,
but qualities to be honored.
Guide us to discover the best within ourselves
and the strengths within our marriage.
We ask this, as we ask all things,
in Jesus' name
and in the power of your Holy Spirit.
Amen.

SCRIPTURE READING: RUTH 1:16–17

For Married Couples

Loving God,
as we confront issues in our marriage
and work out the details of our life together,
we pray for your guidance.
You came to us in a simple way,
to a simple woman, Mary.
Help us to remember
that it is in the simple details of life
that we find you.
As we come together,
bringing with us our different backgrounds
and experiences,
we pray for your presence.
Help us to remember
that you are with us now.
We can see signs of your presence
in all aspects of our lives.
We pray that we can appreciate
all that we have,
our love for one another,
and the love of our family and friends.

"…my cup overflows.
Surely goodness and mercy shall follow me
all the days of my life,

and I shall dwell in the house of the LORD
my whole life long."
Amen.

SCRIPTURE READING: PSALM 23:5–6

For Married Couples

Lord, how do we come to our fullness,
in each other and in you?
How do we continue to grow in love,
with each other and in you?
How can we live this sacrament of marriage
as a sign to one another and to the world?
In your Word,
we hear of your deep love for us.
Help us to see your love in our spouse
each and every day.
Enable us to strengthen each other,
to live out your Word,
to live out your Covenant,
to live out your promise of faithfulness.
Continue to challenge us to grow and to love.
Amen.

SCRIPTURE READING: EPHESIANS 3:16–19

Reaching Out

✦

Making Room at the Table

O loving God, you nourish and sustain us.
We thank you for the gift of food,
which nourishes life.
You continue to be with us
in so many wonderful and marvelous ways,
nourishing and sustaining us always
with food that gives life to all the aspects
of our being.
Help us to use the many ways
in which you nourish us
as sources of unity and life
for all of your people.
Allow us to grow in sensitivity
to the plight of those who are hungry,
alone, frightened, shut out, uninvited,
unwelcome.

May we continually make room for them at
our table,
both in our homes and in our Church.
We pray this in Jesus' name
and in the power of the Holy Spirit.
Amen.

SCRIPTURE READING: MARK 14:12–16, 22–26

Loving God in Others

We long to proclaim our love for you,
O Father,
but mere words are not enough.
Grace us with the courage
to live in love with one another
that in so doing we will truly love you
in the faces of our brothers and sisters.
We are one body in Jesus.
Renew our spirits
so we will learn to love and care
for Christ's body—
feeding the hungry,
clothing the naked,
giving drink to the thirsty,
liberating the captives,

embracing the unwanted, unborn, sick,
and elderly,
healing the hurts
that separate and divide us from one another.
Through the power of your Holy Spirit
and in Jesus' name,
we pray.
Amen.

SCRIPTURE READING: MATTHEW 22:34–40

For Compassion

Mary, you stood at the foot of the cross
and ached with the suffering
your only Child was enduring.
Please help us open our eyes and hearts
and hands
to those children of God
suffering in our midst.
Thank you for nurturing
a compassionate heart in your Son, Jesus,
and help us nurture compassionate hearts
in the children in our lives.

Jesus, help us stand with people,
as you did,

when they are victimized or vilified
because of their sexual orientation,
their race or nationality,
a disease they have,
or criminal deeds they have done.

Help us, O gracious God,
become good neighbors to all your children.
Help us to become sisters and brothers,
in deeds as well as in words,
and advance the coming
of your beloved community.
We pray in the name of your Son, Jesus,
who lives and reigns with you
and the Holy Spirit,
one God, forever and ever.
Amen.

SCRIPTURE READING: LUKE 10:25–37

For Women in the Church

Jesus, your example of praising women
and including them in your ministry
is a challenging one for us these days.
Send us your Spirit of inclusive love
to break open our narrow thinking
and our exclusionary behavior.

Help us to be like the woman
who anointed your feet.
Above all, let it be our love
that humbly and persistently speaks
to those whose rigidity
continues to wound persons deeply
and wound the Church as well.
Jesus, you spoke hard words
when you said you came to sow division,
not peaceful conformity.
Help us to embrace this hard love
and work tirelessly
on behalf of your prophetic words and witness.
We pray, as always, in your name,
Jesus, our Christ and our brother.
Amen.

SCRIPTURE READING: LUKE 7:36–50

For Tender Hearts

God, ever near to us,
your tenderness toward us
is so clear when we hear Jesus assure Jairus,
and address the nameless woman
as "daughter."
May they inspire us to approach you
with such bold humility and faith.
Enlarge our hearts
that in our ministry
we would imitate Jesus in his compassion
for people in all stations of society.
Break down the barriers of fear
that keep us from serving those
who are considered "unclean."
And keep us focused on the work
you set before us, that by our touch,
your touch will be felt.
In Jesus' name we offer you
our hands and hearts.
Amen.

SCRIPTURE READING: MARK 5:21–43

To Be Good Stewards

Compassionate and merciful God,
you adorn the earth with lush treasures
and clothe it in royal attire.
You provide human beings
with every good gift
and you feed us with spiritual food.
Your compassion is endless;
your mercy flows freely like a river.
Gift us, your faithful servants,
with your wisdom and creativity,
so we may be good stewards
of the wealth you have entrusted to our care.
Strengthen us as we go forth
to share your truth with the rest of the world.
Grant this through your Son,
our Lord Jesus Christ,
who lives and reigns with you
and the Holy Spirit,
one God, forever and ever.
Amen.

SCRIPTURE READING: LUKE 16:1–13

Celebrating Diversity

Father of all peoples,
we give thanks for the rich variety
of our human family.
Help us to rejoice in and celebrate
our various racial and cultural heritages.
We give thanks
that you call us to be one family.
In the midst of diversity and discord,
show us our essential unity
as your children.
Form our minds and hearts
so that our differences may become gifts
we offer one another in love.
Amen.

SCRIPTURE READING: GALATIANS 3:26–29

Remembering Others

Leader: Let us lift up our prayers to God
in a spirit of faith and trust.

For those who suffer under the weight
of physical pain or emotional hurt,
that they will experience comfort
and healing,
we pray to the Lord.

All: Lord, hear our prayer.
Leader: For those who serve others humbly,
    in homes, hospitals, prisons, schools,
    and places of worship,
    that they will be strengthened
    in their work,
    we pray to the Lord.
All: Lord, hear our prayer.
Leader: For those who exercise power
    over others
    through business, military service,
    and public office,
    that they will be given the gift
    of servant leadership,
    we pray to the Lord.
All: Lord, hear our prayer.

Leader: *[Invite the group to offer prayers for*
    specific intentions]

All: Lord, hear our prayer.
Leader: We lift up these prayers to you,
    God of mercy and justice.
    Give us the strength and the courage
    to seek true greatness
    through our willingness to serve others.
    Help us with our own struggles
    and ease the pain in our lives.

We ask this in the name of Jesus,
the Suffering Servant
whom we seek to follow.
All: Amen.

SCRIPTURE READING: MARK 10:35–45

For Courage to Act

Dear Lord,
open our hearts to the needs of your world.
Give us the courage
to reach out beyond our comfortable lives
and to look into the suffering faces
of your people.
We are grateful
for the abundance of blessings
you have given us.
We thank you
for your continued love and mercy.
Strengthen us to act
as your instruments of caring
in a world where injustice
and a disregard for the sacred human dignity
of every person is often the rule.

Help us to truly be the salt of the earth
and the light of the world
reaching out in the name of Jesus our Lord.
Amen.

SCRIPTURE READING: MATTHEW 5:13–16

For Greater Gentleness

God of gentleness, compassionate Father,
we offer our time together as a prayer.
We ask that you shower your graces upon us.
We are, at times, unconscious
of our own ability to be violent.
We desire to become more conscious
of the ways
we can act with greater gentleness
so that we may be clearer signs
of your love in our world.
We ask this in Jesus' name,
and through the power of the Holy Spirit.
Amen.

SCRIPTURE READING: JOHN 10:1–5

For Harmony With Others

Spirit of hope within us,
kindle a fire of transforming energy
so great
that our desire for an earth at one with you
consumes us.
We know it is your will
that all of your creation exists in harmony.
Help us, in this moment,
to attend to one another
so that we will be more attentive to you.
Draw us closer to you
through the interaction
we have with one another.
Amen.

SPIRITUAL READING: PHILIPPIANS 3:12–16

For Loving Hearts

O God, whose generous love we receive,
create in us hearts ready for your vineyard,
and hands able to work for you.
Guide us to understand your call,
to desire your will,
and to go to work when you invite us.
Send your Spirit into our lives

to make us loving women and men,
so your reign will be established
on earth as in heaven.
Amen.

SCRIPTURE READING: MATTHEW 20:1–16A

In Times of Violence

God, our Father, we pray
for all victims of violence in relationships.
We especially pray for all women
who have suffered physical
and emotional abuse
at the hands of a loved one.
We pray for children who have witnessed
these horrific acts of violence.
We pray that abusers realize
they have a problem for which
they must seek help,
and we pray that they find the strength
to seek that help.
We pray for special blessings
on all those who minister
to victims of domestic violence.
Lastly, we pray that our Church may lead
the way to working toward peace
in our hopes and our relationships.

Domestic violence thrives on silence.
Lord, let our voices break the silence
and allow us to be "channels of your peace."
Amen.

SCRIPTURE READING: ROMANS 12:9–13

For the Lonely

Lord, we know we are called to be apostles,
laborers for your harvest.
We have been blessed in so many ways,
most importantly
with the gift of faith.
Help us always to be aware
of all those who suffer daily,
especially those who are
without the loving support
of family and friends.
Strengthen us
to be your compassionate hands and heart,
unafraid to share our lives and our faith
in you.
We ask this in your name.
Amen.

SCRIPTURE READING: MATTHEW 9:36–10:8

The Demands of Baptism

For this antiphonal prayer, divide the group into two parts.

Side 1: God of love, in the Jordan River you revealed Jesus as your beloved Son.

Side 2: We praise you for the gift of Christ, our salvation and our peace.

Side 1: You anointed Jesus for the service of the world.

Side 2: Strengthen the Church's witness to this mission in our world today.

Side 1: You brought us to new life and made us members of Christ's Body in baptism.

Side 2: May the gift of your Holy Spirit keep us ready to meet the demands of our baptism.

Side 1: Glory be to the Father, and to the Son, and to the Holy Spirit,

Side 2: As it was in the beginning, is now and will be forever. Amen.

Side 1: The Word became flesh, alleluia!

Side 2: And dwelt among us, alleluia!

SCRIPTURE READING: MARK 1:7–11

On the Beatitudes

For this prayer, invite two people to serve as readers.

Leader: Let us take time to pray together
reflecting on
the spirit of the Beatitudes.
May it be a time to reflect upon ways
to hold ourselves and others to the faith
we profess in Jesus Christ.

Reader 1: Blessed are those who hunger and
thirst for righteousness

Reader 2: ...for they will be satisfied.

All: Generous God, bless those
who are zealous
in their quest for justice and keep them
on a path that is always directed
toward you.
Fill them and us with a desire to
see your "little ones" cared for
and treated with dignity and respect.

Reader 1: Blessed are the merciful
Reader 2: ...for they will be shown mercy.
All: Merciful God, bless those
    who recognize your steadfast love
    in all aspects of their lives and
    who extend themselves to others
    in gentle acts of mercy and compassion.
    Bring them and us comfort
    when we feel most desperate and alone.
Reader 1: Blessed are the clean of heart
Reader 2: ...for they will see God.
All: All-powerful God, bless those
    who are fervent in their faith.
    Reveal yourself to them and to us
    through every aspect of our lives.
Leader: We offer these prayers
    with confidence
    through the Holy Spirit and
    in the name of our Lord, Jesus.
All: Amen.

SCRIPTURE READING: MARK 9:38–43, 45, 47–48

Struggling to Be Just

Lord, Jesus,
how do we find our way in this culture
that throws obstacles constantly
into our path?
Perhaps, as we ponder your Word,
we will come to understand better
our place and our task.
Help us to try our best to be loving, just,
and fair;
help us to bring your example
into our own lives,
into our marriage, and into our community.
Amen.

SCRIPTURE READING: MATTHEW 5:1–12

For the Media

Creator of the world,
inspire us to use modern communication
to unite the human family.
Help us delete the media's prejudices
from our thoughts and actions.
And give us the courage to include
your Word in America's message.
Bless those in the communication media

that they may lead us to high ideals
for candidates and government.
Help them to share truths that will inspire
the human spirit,
bond us as your children,
and motivate lives of worth and generosity.
Amen.

SCRIPTURE READING: MATTHEW 8:24–27

For the Media

All: God, you sent your Word
to dwell among us.
Help us to be open to that same Word
and to the words we hear and read.
Give us sincere, discerning hearts
that we may seek and know the truth.
Motivate us to participate intelligently
in civic life.
May our efforts help to create
a more just world.
Leader: Enlighten anchor persons,
commentators, and producers
to seek and present the truth.
All: Hear us, O Lord.

Leader: Inspire reporters, editors,
     and publishers
     to cover in depth those issues
     that should be brought to our attention.
All: Hear us, O Lord.
Leader: Encourage radio hosts
     to concentrate on the issues
     and not demonize the persons
     involved in the issues.
All: Hear us, O Lord.
Leader: Motivate us to talk about the news
     of the day
     and to respond to that news
     in a compassionate and concrete way.
All: Hear us, O Lord.
Leader: Help us to focus on the issues
     and not get caught up in sensationalism
     or gossip about the personalities
     of government.
All: Hear us, O Lord.
Leader: Give us the discernment
     to critically listen, watch,
     and read the news
     with the gospel in mind.
All: Hear us, O Lord.

Leader: Grant us the energy and courage
    to do what is right and just
    for all your people,
    our brothers and sisters.
All: Hear us, O Lord.
    Amen.

SCRIPTURE READING: MATTHEW 25:3–46

The Presence of God

Heavenly Father, you created
all peoples of every nation
in your image and likeness.
Open our eyes
to the strength of your love for all people.
Open our minds
to your intervention
in every pressing human situation
and social issue.
Give us the humility and discernment
to enter into your love, mercy, justice,
and patience
for all humanity.
Open our hearts
to your compassionate understanding.
Show us where to begin.

We ask this through your Son, Jesus,
our Lord and brother.
Amen.

SCRIPTURE READING: MATTHEW 25:31–46

Accepting Our Gifts

Lord Jesus,
you healed the sick,
brought the lost sheep home,
gave the abandoned hope.
You offered a welcome to all.
Well into the night you heard laughter
around your supper table,
where you made those without confidence
stand tall.
You loved and respected everyone.
You accepted those who made mistakes
and let you down.
You were straightforward with all.
Above all, you wanted everyone
to join in the harvest
that you knew would come,
in spite of great evil and death,
the harvest that would be a hundredfold.
Thank you, Jesus,

for sharing with us your life and love,
for helping us to see
that we all have gifts and abilities,
for showing us why our work can be good.
Amen.

SCRIPTURE READING: GENESIS 1:26–31

Remembering Others

Leader: Let us pray.
   For peace in the world,
All: Lord, have mercy.
Leader: For those who are in prison
   for the sake of justice,
All: Lord, have mercy.
Leader: For those who suffer
   because of natural disasters,
All: Lord, have mercy.
Leader: For those who are sick
   because of pollution,
All: Lord, have mercy.
Leader: For those who are upset
   because of their fear for the future,
All: Lord, have mercy.

Leader: For children who are abused
    in their homes or place of work,
All: Lord, have mercy.
Leader: For those who forget us,
All: Lord, have mercy.
Leader: For those who love and hate us,
All: Lord, have mercy.
    Amen.

SCRIPTURE READING: LUKE 21:5–19

Welcoming Others

Lord Jesus,
you showed how dear human life is to you:
our health through your healings;
our sense of belonging
and being accepted
through your welcome to outcasts;
our sense of making a difference
and being valued
through your good news.
As members of your Church,
we want to share with you
in bringing this love of life to others.

Help us to care more deeply
about the ways we welcome
and celebrate others—
all others—in our midst.
Amen.

SCRIPTURE READING: 1 TITUS 3:8–9, 14

Living the Gospel

All: Gracious God, we thank you
for the challenge of your Word
and the support of this community.
We place our needs before you,
trusting that you hear us
and respond to us with compassion
and wisdom.

Leader: Let us offer our prayers of petition.
For those who suffer the injustice of …

[Invite people to name specific injustices.]

All: Lord, hear our prayer.

Leader: For those who are poor because they
lack…

[Invite specific petitions.]

All: Lord, hear our prayer.

Leader: For those who are oppressed by …

[Invite specific petitions.]

All: Lord, hear our prayer.
Leader: For these people,
　　for all of our loved ones,
　　and the intentions we hold in our hearts,
　　we pray to the Lord.
All: Lord, hear our prayer.
　　Holy God, inspire our hearts
　　by the grace of your Holy Spirit,
　　that we may offer you
　　the praise of seeking ways
　　to act justly,
　　love tenderly,
　　and walk humbly with You.
　　Amen.

SCRIPTURE READING: MICAH 6:6–8

The Work of the Gospel

Gracious God,
in Jesus' words
we are invited to be partners
in his work of witnessing to your kingdom
on earth.
In his words,

we are reminded of the mission
and responsibility
that we received in our baptism.
Keep our hearts, eyes, and ears open,
so that daily we will respond to your call.
With courage and humility,
relying on your grace,
may we be agents of healing,
bearers of truth, and messengers of hope.
We offer this prayer through Jesus Christ
our Lord.
Amen.

SCRIPTURE READING: MARK 6:7–13

Day by Day

God of all times, you give us days to work
and days to rest from our labors.
Help us to follow your Son,
the master of the Sabbath,
who taught us to see in each day
the opportunity to serve one another
in charity.
We ask this through the same Christ our Lord.
Amen.

SCRIPTURE READING: MARK 2:23–3:6

Letting Go

ᕙᕗ

To Live in the Present

Lord, help us to remember
that time is not a possession.
We cannot "have time."
We cannot "waste time."
We cannot "spend time."
We cannot "save time."
We cannot "steal time."
We cannot "use time."
We cannot even "give time."
It is all an illusion.
Time was never ours.
It slips through our lives
like sand through an hourglass,
completely beyond our control.
Protect us from letting it become a tyrant
that wastes, spends, and steals our energies.

Help us to remember the only moment
we have is NOW.
We are called to be in it,
truly present to you and to each other,
to feel with and for the others,
and to find,
in that peaceful presence,
protection against the hostility and violence
of our hurrying hearts.
Remind us, Lord,
there is a time for everything,
every season under heaven.
Amen.

SCRIPTURE READING: ECCLESIASTES 3:1–8

To Grow in Faith

All: I prayed, and understanding was given me;
I called on God, and the spirit of wisdom
came to me (Wisdom 7:7).

Leader: Father, Creator and giver of life,
help us to embrace the gifts you have
given to us and show us how to use them
generously in service to your people.

All: I prayed, and understanding was given me;
I pleaded, and the spirit of Wisdom came
to me.

Leader: Jesus, Savior and Redeemer,
show us how to let go
of those aspects of our lives
that inhibit our growth,
make us timid and fearful,
and keep us from seeing
the larger possibilities that lie before us.

All: I prayed, and understanding was given me;
I pleaded, and the spirit of Wisdom came
to me.

Leader: Spirit of wisdom and love,
fill our hearts with passion for your word
and a zealousness for your work.

All: I prayed, and understanding was given me;
I pleaded, and the spirit of Wisdom came
to me.

Leader: May all good things come to us
as a result of Wisdom's company
and true riches be ours
through God's abundant grace.

All: Glory to the Father,
and to the Son,
and to the Holy Spirit,
as it was in the beginning, is now,
and will be forever.
Amen.

SCRIPTURE READING: MARK 10:17–30

We Are Called

Jesus, we did not choose you.
Rather, you chose us
to go forth as emissaries of God's love
and peace
into every part and place of our lives.
What an awesome calling—
to be your eyes, your ears, your hands
for others.
Free us from the selfishness
and fears that hold us back.
Still us at the beginning of each day,
so that we may hear your voice
and feel your love blessing us
and sending us forth.
Open us to the giftedness
of those with whom we minister,
and help us become more attentive
and supportive allies.
All of these blessings we ask in your name,
as you told us to,
you who live and reign
with the Father and the Holy Spirit,
one God, forever and ever.
Amen.

SCRIPTURE READING: LUKE 10:1–9

We Are Invited

Lord God,
in your wisdom you invite us
out of our complacency.
You open our eyes
to see you with new vision.
You open our hearts
to love you with greater passion,
and you open our hands
to serve you with the purest intentions.
Lead us more deeply
into the mystery of discipleship,
so that we may follow you
with steadfast faithfulness.
Give us the heart of Mary,
so that we may be transformed
by your Word
and fortified by your presence.
Give us the mind of Martha,
so that we can diligently accomplish
your mission.
But, above all, continue to invite us
into intimate and lasting relationship.
We ask this through Christ, our Lord.
Amen.

SCRIPTURE READING: LUKE 10:38–42

Listening to Our Hearts

Loving and generous Father,
You alone know the workings
of the human heart.
Show us how to listen to the yearnings
we have deep within ourselves.
Remove from our midst any impediments
or distractions
that block us from turning to you in our need.
Open us up to your healing touch
and your bounteous goodness.
Then we shall be free to rejoice,
along with those faithful ones of ages past,
in your generosity
and in your power to heal and console.
We offer this prayer and all of our deepest needs
in the name of your Son, our Lord Jesus Christ.
Amen.

SCRIPTURE READING: MARK 10:46–52

Sharing the World's Bounty

Lord, God of heaven and earth,
the gift of life that you have shared with us
is sustained and nurtured by the world
in which we live.

If we, as your human family,
cherish our world and learn to share its goods,
there will be enough for us all,
not just to survive but to thrive.
Purify us, O Lord,
of the greed and selfishness
that anxiously drive us to acquire
that which we really don't need,
and misuse or deplete
that which others may require to survive.
Teach us, O Lord,
that we are valued for who we are in your sight,
and not for what we have
in the eyes of others.
Bless us with a generous spirit
and a servant's heart,
that you may rejoice in having entrusted
this world, our home, to our safekeeping.
May you be praised by how we treat the earth
and one another.
Hear us, through Jesus, your Son,
who walked our land,
lived in our world,
and gave his life that all may be transformed
and given as gift to you, now and forever.
Amen.

SCRIPTURE READING: ROMANS 8:18–25

In the Midst of Busyness

God of compassion,
we pray for a new heart.
We know that our hearts
need your touch.
Often, we let our busyness
get in the way
of our relationship with you.
Enlighten our minds,
so that we may truly be
the persons of peace
you desire us to be.
Give us strength to carry out,
with gentleness,
our resolve to change in some small way.
We call ourselves your followers in name;
we resolve to be that in action.
We depend on you for help.
In confidence and faith, we pray.
Amen.

SCRIPTURE READING: MATTHEW 6:5–14; 26:47–56

Lenten Desert

For this antiphonal prayer, divide the group into two parts.

Side 1: God of the Covenant, just as your Spirit
   sent Jesus into the wilderness, so you have
   sent us, your people, into the desert of Lent.

Side 2: Doubtful and fearful we come,
   confused by the whirlwind pace
   of our lives
   and the clamor of lesser voices.

Side 1: Yet we long for the simplicity
   and strength
   of a life centered in you, O God,
   source of our joy and our peace.

Side 2: Help us to enter the desert of Lent,
   and, leaving all else aside,
   let us rest in you alone.

All: Amen.

SCRIPTURE READING: MARK 1:12–15

In Times of Loss

Our Father, we are gathered here
as grieving people,
as people who are lost.
We are looking for your dwelling place.
We pray that you will send your Spirit
to accompany us on this journey,
so that we are able to see hope.
In our time of loss or trouble,
help us discover new rituals for our lives.
Guide us as you will, so that we
may have new life in you.
We ask this in Jesus' name
and in the power of the Holy Spirit.
Amen.

SCRIPTURAL READING: PSALM 27:1, 4–5
OR ISAIAH 43:1, 2

In Times of Suffering

Leader: Lord God, our crosses are heavy,
more than we seem able to bear at times.
We believe that you have not turned away
from us in our struggle to be faithful.
Hear us and be our help
as we place our needs before you.

All: "It is the Lord GOD who helps me;
     who will declare me guilty?" (Isaiah 50:9)

Leader: It is tempting at times,
     like Peter, to deny
     the suffering that is part of our growth
     in faith.
     Give us the courage to accept our crosses
     with hope and grace.

All: The Lord God is my help;
     who will prove me wrong?

Leader: Sometimes it is harder to watch others
     struggle under the weight of their crosses
     than to bear our own.
     Show us how to be supportive, caring, and
     compassionate with those who are in pain.

All: The Lord God is my help;
     who will prove me wrong?

Leader: The invitation to save our lives
     through losing them
     is both mysterious and disturbing.
     Strengthen us as we let go of aspects
     of living
     that ultimately rob us of true life in you.

All: The Lord God is my help;
     who will prove me wrong?

Leader: We ask all of this in the name of Jesus,
     our Lord and Savior.

All: The Lord God is my help;
who will prove me wrong?
Amen.

SCRIPTURE READING: MARK 8:27–35

Freedom From Unreasonable Worries

Lord, you came to set us free,
but our materialism
threatens to enslave us.
Give us the strength we need
to confront our own unreasonable desires
and those of our families.
Help us to take to heart your command
not to worry about what we are to eat
or what we are to put on.

*[Invite each member of the group to mention one
materialistic worry from which he or she would
like to be freed, using the following words:]*

Free me especially from worry about…

Leader: Let us pray together the prayer Jesus
gave us for all our needs.
All: Our Father…

SCRIPTURE READING: LUKE 16:19–31

Asking Forgiveness

◉━◇◇◇━◉

Repentance

Leader: Loving and gentle God, for the times we have been insensitive to the needs of others,

All: Lord, we repent and believe in the Good News.

Leader: For the times we have not resisted evil, but have given in to it instead,

All: Lord, we repent and believe in the Good News.

Leader: For the times we have failed to offer hope and support,

All: Lord, we repent and believe in the Good News.

Leader: For the times we have shut ourselves off from comfort, hope, and support,

All: Lord, we repent and believe in the Good
News.

Leader: For the times we have allowed
cynicism to reign,

All: Lord, we repent and believe in the Good
News.

Leader: Loving God, we turn to you in love
and trust.
Allow your reign to grow continually in
our hearts,
now and always.

All: Amen.

SCRIPTURE READING: MARK 1:14–20

Repentance

Leader: For the times, Lord,
when we have resisted
responding to the needs
of those who are beginning life anew,
we say, "Lord have mercy."

All: Lord, have mercy.

Leader: For the times when we have
neglected to reach out
because we were preoccupied
with our lives

and failed to recognize the vulnerability
of another,
we say, "Christ have mercy."

All: Christ, have mercy.

Leader: For the times when we have failed
to prevent the shaming of another
through acts of protective concern, charity,
or sharing our resources,
we say, "Lord have mercy."

All: Lord, have mercy.

Leader: We surrender to you,
God of great generosity.
Guide our actions, our attitudes,
and our attentiveness so that we may see
when to say yes to your call
through those who struggle around us.
We pray this in Jesus' name.

All: Amen.

SCRIPTURE READING: JOHN 2:1–11

In Advent

Leader: O loving God, You promised to send
     your Son, Jesus,

All: Make ready the way of the Lord!

Leader: You forgive us our failings each day,

All: Make ready the Way of the Lord!

Leader: You came as the least among us,

All: Make ready the way of the Lord!

Leader: You ask us to forgive others as you
     forgive us,

All: Make ready the way of the Lord!

Leader: With your support we will care for
     those we've neglected,

All: Make ready the way of the Lord!

Leader: Be with us on our journey,

All: Make ready the way of the Lord!

All: O God, our Father,
     as your prophet John the Baptist
     instructs us,
     we ask not only your forgiveness
     but your loving help
     that we may turn away from being satisfied
     and complacent with our present lives,
     and make our every living day
     a prayer of praise and thanksgiving to you
     by our attitudes and by our actions.

We ask this through your Son,
Jesus Christ, in union with the Holy Spirit.
Amen.

SCRIPTURE READING: LUKE 3:1–6

For Trust in God

Leader: For all the times, Lord, when we have
put our desire for money and possessions
above our relationship with you, we pray,

All: Lord, have mercy.

Leader: For all the times we have considered
ourselves better than others because of our
wealth or education, we pray,

All: Lord, have mercy.

Leader: For all the times we have been selfish
and turned away from the needs of others,
we pray,

All: Lord, have mercy.

Leader: For all the times we have worried
over what we would eat, drink, or wear,
we pray,

All: Lord, have mercy.

Leader: For all the times we have been self-
righteous, we pray,

All: Lord, have mercy upon us.

Leader: For all the times we have judged
   others according to outward appearances,
   we pray,
All: Lord, have mercy upon us.
Our Father…

SCRIPTURE READING: MATTHEW 6:24–34

For New Perspectives

For this antiphonal prayer, divide the group into
two parts.

Side 1: We are loved by our God,
   yet we often love poorly.
   Show us the way, Lord.
Side 2: You have made us your sisters
   and brothers,
   yet we often ignore the crosses
   of our sisters and brothers
   in God's human family.
   Show us the way, Lord.
Side 1: Although you accept us as we are,
   we often do not accept others or ourselves.
   Show us the way, Lord.

Side 2: You have showered upon us
life's blessings,
yet we often refuse to help the needy.
Show us the way, Lord.

All: Dear God, give us a new perspective.
Help us look at the world
through the eyes of Jesus the Christ,
and be truly willing to take up our crosses
and follow him.
Amen.

SCRIPTURE READING: MATTHEW 10:37–42

For Change in Ourselves and Society

Faithful and loving God and Father,
we come to you as people
in need of conversion.
We long for a more simple way
of living on the earth.
Our hearts,
so filled with the many activities of the day,
now stop to beg for your light and wisdom.
We want to be your instruments
of peace in our world.

We desire to make changes in ourselves
and to advocate for changes in those systems
that may cause violence in our society.
We ask this through Jesus,
who lives and reigns with you
and the Holy Spirit forever and ever.
Amen.

SCRIPTURE READING: LUKE 4:14–21

For Integrity

Merciful God,
forgive us the times we enter
into worship with ill tempers
and self-righteous attitudes.
When we lose sight of the purpose
for our external practices,
challenge us to examine the disposition
of our hearts.
Help us to grow in integrity
that in all our actions
your justice and grace will be known.
With grateful hearts
we offer our prayer through Christ our Lord.
Amen.

SCRIPTURE READING: MARK 7:1–8, 14–15, 21–23

Both Sides

God of mercy,
at one time or another
we have all been on both sides
of rejection and misunderstanding.
Where we need to forgive,
please give us the grace to do so.
Where we need to seek forgiveness,
please give us the courage to seek it.
With single-minded commitment,
help us to do the work
to which we are called,
even as we face challenging situations.
Help us to be open to the prophets
in our own midst,
so we do not fail to hear your voice
in the ones with whom we live, work,
and worship.
In Jesus' name we pray.
Amen.

SCRIPTURE READING: MARK 6:1–6

Work

Leader: For the opportunity to find work meaningful,

All: We thank you, God.

Leader: For those with whom we work,

All: We ask your blessing, God.

Leader: For the times we were not conscious of our partnership with you,

All: We ask forgiveness, O God.

Leader: For those who have taught us skills and wisdom and patience,

All: We praise you, O God.

SCRIPTURE READING: COLOSSIANS 1:9–12

Prayers to Mary

❧❧

RENEW Prayer to Mary

Mary, you are a woman
wrapped in silence
and yet the Word born of your yes
continues to bring life to all creation.
Mary, help us to say yes—
to be bearers of good news
to a world waiting.

Mary, you are a virgin and a mother
empowered by the Holy Spirit.
Help us to open ourselves
to that same life-bringing Spirit.
Mary, help us to say our yes.

Mary, you are gift of Jesus to us,
mother of the Church.
Look upon our world and our lives.

Pray for us to your Son
that we might be renewed,
and that we might help renew
the face of the earth.

Mary, help us to say yes.
Amen.

SCRIPTURE READINGS: LUKE 1:38; MATTHEW 1:18–25

Daily Choices

Mary and Joseph,
you said yes to God
when you were faced with difficult choices.
Help and guide us,
in our daily lives, to choose wisely.
May we be able to lead
stronger Christian lives,
based on sound values—
lives that reach beyond our own wants
to the needs of others.
We ask all this
in the name of the God you obeyed,
the Son that you nurtured,
and the Spirit you followed.
Amen.

SCRIPTURE READINGS: LUKE 1:38; MATTHEW 1:18–25

For Compassion

Mary, you saw people in need
and acted.
O compassionate Mother,
help us to open our eyes
to the needs of others
and to respond to what we see.
Help us, in our giving,
to be closer to the model of the widow
than to that of the rich man.
We thank you most of all for giving us
your Son to show us the way.
We pray for all in need
to the heavenly Father,
through the same Christ our Lord.
Amen.

SCRIPTURE READING: LUKE 1:39–45, 56 OR JOHN 2:1–11

For Our Church

O Mary, our Mother,
as a Church we need your guidance
and attention,
but most of all, your example
of sacrificial love.
May we imitate you

in our commitment to serve each other
as members of God's Church
and to respond to the needs of the world.
Teach us to be Church more faithfully,
and live the gospel more completely,
in imitation of Jesus your Son,
who lives and reigns with the Father
and the Holy Spirit forever and ever.
Amen.

SCRIPTURE READING: LUKE 1:46–55
OR ACTS 1:12–14; 2:1–4

For the Suffering

Mary, Mother of Sorrows
and Comforter of the Afflicted,
grant that we may share with you
in the pain of your Son's sufferings.
As you were so fully present
to the agony of your Son,
may we too be present to the pain
and suffering of those in our midst
and, through our compassion and love,
bring to them a measure of consolation,
through the same Christ our Lord.
Amen.

SCRIPTURE READING: LUKE 2:25–35 OR JOHN 19:25–30

For Patience

Mary, Mother of Sorrows,
you share in the pain of the world.
Through patient endurance,
you came to experience the joy
of your Son's Resurrection.
Help us to travel the way of your Son,
to walk with courage,
and to bring healing, comfort,
and understanding
to the world around us.
We ask all of this of God our Father,
through the same Christ our Lord.
Amen.

SCRIPTURE READING: LUKE 2:25–35 OR JOHN 19:25–30

Prayer
Experiences

❦

*"All these were constantly devoting
themselves to prayer."*

ACTS 1:14

Celebrating
God's Love

❧∿❧

Setting: *On a table in the midst of the group, place a bible open to the appropriate Scripture passage, a lighted candle, and a glass bowl filled with holy water.*

Leader: We gather in the presence of our
  Triune God
who is a community of Love.
Let us enter into the peace and energy
  of that love
as we quiet ourselves in the presence of our God.

Action: *Pause for reflection.*

Leader: We begin our time together by
  blessing ourselves in the name of the Father,
  and of the Son, and of the Holy Spirit.

Action: *The bowl of holy water is passed around and each person blesses herself or himself.*

Leader: Let us continue with a reading from Paul's letter to the Ephesians.

Reader: Ephesians 4:1–6

Leader: We will now use words of Saint Paul in his letter to the Ephesians, chapter 3, verses 14 to 20, as a prayer and as a recognition of the promise of what God can do among us.

Reader: I bow my knees before you, Father, from whom every family in heaven and on earth takes its name.

All: Come dwell in our hearts, O God.

Reader: I pray that, according to the riches of your glory, you may grant that we may be strengthened in our inner being with power through your Spirit.

All: Come dwell in our hearts, O God.

Reader: May Christ dwell in our hearts through faith, as we are being rooted and grounded in love.

All: Come dwell in our hearts, O God.

Reader: I pray that we may have the power to comprehend, with all the saints, what are the breadth and length and height and depth of God's love.

All: Come dwell in our hearts, O God.

Reader: May we know the love of Christ that surpasses all knowledge.

All: Come dwell in our hearts, O God.

Reader: May we be filled with all the fullness of God.

All: Come dwell in our hearts, O God.

Reader: To you, Lord Jesus, who by the power of the Holy Spirit at work within us are able to accomplish abundantly more than all we can imagine, to you be glory in the Church.

All: Come dwell in our hearts, O God.

Action: *Allow a pause for reflection.*

Leader: Let us pray together.

All: Glory be to the Father, and to the Son, and to the Holy Spirit.
Amen.

Seeking Forgiveness

✧

Setting: *On the prayer table, place a bowl of stones of various sizes and shapes, a lighted candle and the Bible open to the appropriate reading (see below).*

Reader: Scripture Reading: John 8:3–11

Leader: Lord, it is easy for us to remember the hurts others have inflicted on us. Help us to call to mind the hurts we have inflicted, the stones we have thrown. We know you have forgiven us. Help us to forgive ourselves.

Action: *Invite each person in the group to take a stone to represent a hurt he or she has caused, something for which it has been difficult to forgive him or herself. As each one takes a stone, he or she is to name it with one word, such as "anger," "jealousy," "revenge," and so on. At the naming of each "sin," the response is:*

All: Forgive us, Lord, and help us to forgive ourselves.

Action: *After all members have participated in the litany, pray:*

All: Lord, Jesus Christ, Son of the living God, have mercy on me a sinner.

Leader: We know we must not throw stones at another because we are sinners also. Place your stone someplace where it will serve as a reminder of the need to forgive ourselves, each other, our world.

All: Our Father…

Remembering
the Hungry

⌘

Setting: *On the prayer table, place a lighted candle, a bible open to the appropriate reading (see below), and a container with slips of paper. On each paper is the name of a particular ministry or organization that provides food for the hungry. For instance, the parish soup kitchen, the Society of Saint Vincent de Paul, Catholic Relief Services, Second Harvest.*

Reader: Leviticus 19:9–10, 15, 33–34

Action: *Leader invites each member of the group to choose a slip of paper from the bowl and, one by one, name a group that feeds the hungry. Members may also choose to add a petition for a personal need or hope related to hunger.*

All: We pray for all the people served by these ministries and organizations and we lay

before you, heavenly God, all these needs
and hopes, asking you to respond to them
in the fullness of your love. Through Jesus
Christ our Lord who lives and loves with
you and the Holy Spirit in one loving
community. Amen.

Reader: Leviticus 19:9–10, 15, 33–34

*Action: Allow a few minutes of quiet reflection.
Then ask for people to share their thoughts. At the
end of group sharing:*

All: Thank you, God, for your faithful
servants who give a helping hand to the
hungry. Bless them and those whose pain
and hardship make their work so essential.
Show us how we can stand with them.
Give bread to the hungry and give hunger
for you to those who have bread. We pray
in the name of Jesus our Savior and
brother who feeds us with the bread of life
and who lives in loving community with
you and the Holy Spirit. Amen.

Commissioning
Disciples

⚭

Setting: *This prayer is appropriate for many different occasions in parish ministry.*

Priest: In the name of the Father, and of the Son, and of the Holy Spirit.

All: Amen.

Reader I: The word commission has two parts. The word *mission* means to be sent. The prefix *com* means with or together. So the word commission means to be sent with or together. Jesus was sent by the Father with the power of the Holy Spirit to evangelize the world. The Church is sent by Jesus, with the power of the Spirit, to continue his mission here on earth. The Apostles and their successors were commissioned with the gift of the Holy

Spirit to bring peace to the world through the forgiveness of sins (John 20:19–23). We, as the Church, are called and sent to participate in this mission. Listen to Jesus sending us forth.

Reader II: Matthew 28:16–20

All: Praise to you, Lord Jesus Christ!
We choose to go where you lead us!
Priest: May God complete
the work begun in you,
and keep the Gifts of the Holy Spirit
active in your hearts.
All: Amen.
Priest: May you be ready to live the gospel,
eager to do God's will,
and always enthusiastic
in proclaiming God's Word.
All: Amen.
Priest: May the God of love and peace
abide in you, guide your steps,
and confirm your hearts in his love.
And may Almighty God bless you,
the Father, the Son, and the Holy Spirit.

Action: All make the sign of the cross and respond:

All: Amen.

Celebrating God's Creation

❦

Setting: *On the prayer table, place a bible opened to the appropriate reading, a lighted candle, and symbols of earth and sea. These might include: pine cones, acorns, fresh tomatoes or another seasonal fruit or vegetable, photo of a rainbow, photos of the human family.*

Reader: John 1:1–3

Action: *The leader invites each participant to come to the table and select one item from the collection of symbols. Allow a time for reflection on the individual symbols. Then invite each participant to offer a prayer related to his or her object. It could be a prayer of praise and thanksgiving, of petition, of sorrow. Each person then returns the item to the prayer table. Allow another short pause for reflection.*

Reader: John 1:1–3

Leader: We praise you, Creator God, for all
creation. Teach us to respect and love our
one sacred community.

All: Send forth your Spirit, Lord, and renew
the face of the earth.

Leader: We thank you, Giver of Life, for the
life we share with one another, with you
and with all of creation. Fill our hearts
with even greater gratitude for all
of your gifts.

All: Send forth your Spirit, Lord, and renew
the face of the earth.

Leader: We ask you to forgive us,
Compassionate God, for the times we
failed to reverence your creation.

All: Send forth your Spirit, Lord, and renew
the face of the earth.
Amen.

Honoring Father, Son, and Spirit

⌒⌒⌒⌒

Setting: *On the prayer table, place a bible opened to the appropriate passage, a lighted votive candle, and enough tapers for all participants.*

Action: *Invite each person to approach the table, select a taper, light it from the votive candle, and return to his or her place. If there is a large group, participants approach in pairs.*

Leader: Let us say together slowly and reflectively: "In the name of the Father, and of the Son and of the Holy Spirit. Amen."

Reader: John 14:16–17

Action: *Allow a moment of prayerful silence.*

All: Loving Father, Creator of all,
we surrender our hearts to you this day.
We ask that you write your law within us,
that we may be reflections of your love
to others,
and that as a community of disciples
our Church may always be
the sacrament of your presence
in the world.

Action: *A moment of prayerful silence.*

All: Lord Jesus, Redeemer and Lord,
help us to be your presence in the world.
May our hearts beat with yours,
our hands reach out with your love,
our feet move us
more toward your compassion.
Transform our eyes that we may truly see,
our ears that we may truly listen,
our mouths that we may learn
to speak of your love.
May we grow more and more
in your likeness
as we desire your love to be made visible
in our lives.

Action: *A moment of prayerful silence.*

All: Holy Spirit, Sanctifier,
    we surrender ourselves to you.
    Permeate us, and breathe new life
    into our community.
    Make us temples of your presence,
    and empower us to bear the fruit of faith
    in our lives
    as we respond to your call
    to live in right relationship with all
    whom we encounter.

Action: *A moment of prayerful silence.*

All: Holy triune God, you dwell
    within each of us.
    Help us to know that the light
    of your Presence,
    only symbolized by candles,
    is truly realized in each of us.
    We extinguish our candles
    not to live in darkness,
    but because we have become your light,
    your candles for the world.
    Help us see beyond the false divisions
    that separate us from one another
    so that we may truly live
    as reflections of your love,

as we await the fulfillment of your reign
here on earth,
O God, Father, Son, and Holy Spirit.
Amen.

Action: *Extinguish tapers. If there is time and not too many participants, this can be done individually, one after another.*

Enkindling the Fire
of the Holy Spirit

Setting: *On the prayer table, place a bible, a bowl of holy water, a lighted candle, and as many unlighted tapers as there are participants.*

Action: *A moment of prayerful silence.*

Reader 1: Matthew 28:19–20
Reader 2: Luke 12:49
Reader 3: Ephesians 1:17–18

Action: *The group gathers in a circle around the prayer table. Each participant approaches the table, uses the water in the bowl to sign herself or himself with the cross, lights a taper from the votive candle, and returns to a place in the circle.*

Leader: Lord, enkindle us with the fire
of your Holy Spirit.
Fill us with your love.
Give us hearts that long to spread
the fire of your gospel
throughout the world.
Remind us, Lord, of our own baptism,
our first encounter through water and fire
with your sacramental presence.
Give us the strength to respond
to your promises of new life
and conversion.
Let this water and this fire become signs
of renewed faith.
Make us ever more aware of the presence
of your love in the world.

All: We pray that the fire of the Holy Spirit
may bring more people of our country
to the discipleship of Jesus.

Leader: Lord, as the radiance of the sun
will bend a flower toward its light,
so too does the radiance of your love turn
us toward you.
And yet, unlike the flowers,
we often resist you.
We put up obstacles and barriers
against you.

Although your light draws us near,
we resist and rebel.
And we find ourselves feeling alone.

All: We pray, Lord, that you convert us
once again,
today and every day.
Empower us to turn toward the light
of your love.

Leader: As we, your disciples, gather here,
Lord,
let this community grow
as a sign of your transforming presence
among us.
Let our faith as a community shine bright.
Let us be a source of strength
and encouragement,
hope and joy, peace and justice.
We ask you now to touch the people we
hold close to our hearts,
the ones we long to place in your arms.
Bless them, heal them, touch them.

Action: *A moment of silence to remember those
people for whom participants wish to pray.*

All: God, our Father, let us sow seeds of love
and mercy.

Let us sow the seeds of the gospel
so that the Good News of your Son, Jesus,
will take root throughout the world.
Give us gifts of kindness and respect.
Send your Holy Spirit
with whatever gifts we need
to plant the gospel throughout the world.
Amen.

Action: *All extinguish candles.*